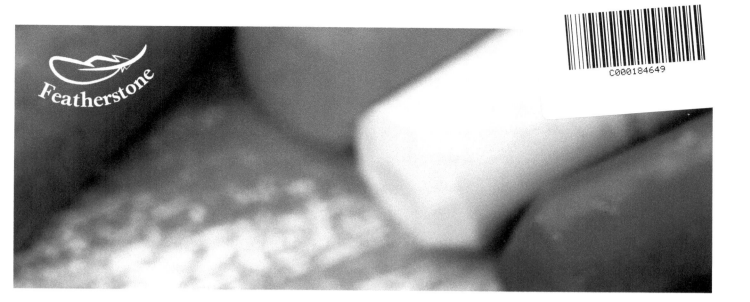

FOUNDATIONS OF
LITERACY

A balanced approach to language, listening and literacy skills in the Early Years

Fully revised for the new EYFS

Sue Palmer and **Ros Bayley**
with contributions from **Lynn Broadbent**

Featherstone

Published 2013 by Featherstone,
an imprint of Bloomsbury Publishing plc,
50 Bedford Square, London, WC1B 3DP
www.bloomsbury.com

First published 2004 by Continuum International Publishing Group

ISBN 978-1-4081-9384-6

Text © Sue Palmer
Design © Lynda Murray
Photographs © Shutterstock: pages 4, 11, 13, 14, 16, 17, 22, 29, 30, 32, 33, 39,
42, 43, 46, 49, 56, 57, 58, 61, 62, 63, 65, 66, 68, 69, 73, 74, 76, 77, 78, 88, 90,
92, 96, 98, 99, 102, 103, 105, 115, 118, 125, 127, 134, 135, 136.

Printed by CPI Group (UK) Ltd, Croydon, CR0 4YY

Typeset by Fakenham Prepress Solutions, Fakenham, Norfolk, NR21 8NN

10 9 8 7 6 5 4 3 2 1

This book is produced using paper that is made from wood grown in
managed, sustainable forests. It is natural, renewable and recyclable.
The logging and manufacturing processes conform to the environmental
regulations of the country of origin.

To see our full range of titles visit www.bloomsbury.com

Contents

About the authors

Sue Palmer, a former primary headteacher, has written more than 200 books and educational television programmes on aspects of literacy and acted as a literacy consultant to the National Literacy Strategy, National Literacy Trust, many educational publishers and the BBC. Research for her books on child development in the modern world (Toxic Childhood, Detoxing Childhood, 21st Century Boys and 21st Century Girls), led to a profound interest in the significance of play in children's learning, and collaboration with Ros Bayley on the *Foundations of Literacy* project. She lives in Scotland, where she is currently a member of the Scottish government's Early Years Task Force.

Following an extensive career as an early years teacher, Ros Bayley became well-known as an early years consultant, trainer and storyteller. Throughout her career she devoted much time to developing children's creativity and imagination through story, puppetry, music, dance and dramatic play, and shared her strategies with practitioners both in the UK and abroad. She also had a passionate interest in the development of literacy skills and wrote a wide range of resources for foundation stage practitioners. She was a contributor to the DfES Curriculum Guidance for the Foundation Stage. Ros's tragically early death in 2012 deprived us all of a great teacher and advocate of young children's right to play.

Lynn Broadbent started her career as a teacher, working with Ros Bayley, and collaborated with her constantly during the 40 years of their friendship. Together they produced more than 20 books and teaching materials, on language, literacy, creativity and personal, social and emotional development. Lynn has worked for many years as an Early Years Adviser and is now an Early Years Consultant.

Acknowledgements

The authors would like to thank the many early years practitioners, primary teachers and other professionals who have helped in the compilation of this book, throughout the U.K. and Europe. Special thanks are due to Pie Corbett (literacy), Linda Caroe (music), and Clare Mills and Philippa Crooks (speech and language), who contributed so much to our understanding and have given us many new ideas. We are also particularly grateful to the following people for advice and/or support: Margaret Donaldson; Roger Beard; Greg Brooks; Anne Locke; Diane Hofkins; Julia Bond; Carole Kimberley; David Mills; Sue Moncur and Janet King; Paul Hanbury; Peter Brinton, Mandy Lawrence, Catherine Williams, Claire Taylor, Jo Small and Pat Hart of Roskear Primary School, Cornwall; Hazel Mills and the children and staff of Arkwright Nursery and Lady Bay School in Nottingham; Manor Park Primary School, Acorn Childcare Ltd, London Early Years Foundation for the latest photographs and Michaela Morgan for permission to use rhymes co-written with Sue Palmer. We should also like to thank the National Literacy Trust for bringing Sue and Ros together to present some conferences and Child Education magazine for commissioning the series of articles that inspired the book.

Foreword

The Introduction to the first edition of this book was jointly written by me, Sue Palmer (a literacy specialist with an interest in early years) and my friend Ros Bayley (an early years specialist with an interest in literacy). We'd got together in response to concern among early years practitioners that, in a multi-media world, children's language and listening skills were less well-honed than in the past. At the same time, the 'academic' demands of early education had increased – so, as oral language development became ever more important, less and less time was available for it.

Our aim was to provide advice about the developmental foundations of literacy that was easily accessible, based on best practice from the UK and Europe, and – above all – fun. We agreed that, since play is the natural human learning drive, the more fun an activity is, the more likely it is to enhance learning. So we devised a seven-stranded 'fun-packed' approach to covering the developmental foundations of literacy learning.

The idea was to combine information about the 'what' and 'why' of these developmental foundations with plenty of child-friendly starting points for 'how'. Each chapter therefore consists of research-based pages (for which I took major responsibility) and practical pages (which mostly came from Ros). However, as time went on, we found our contributions constantly overlapping – nothing about teaching and learning is ever straightforward!

It was enormous fun working together – it always felt more like play than work – so when the book was finished we hoped it would prove both accessible and useful to practitioners. Never in our wildest dreams did we expect that almost ten years later there would be demand for a fourth edition… Nor did we imagine there would be only one of us here to write the new Introduction.

Ros became ill early in 2012, shortly after our publisher asked us to update *Foundations of Literacy* to fit the requirements of the revised Early Years Foundation Stage (EYFS). Talking over the new edition, we concluded that – although much has changed in the world of early education – best practice doesn't change much at all. Indeed, over the last ten years, there's been copious research to back up our original conviction that the soundest foundations for literacy are an active, play-based curriculum, an emphasis on oral learning, and plenty of time for music, movement, song and stories. Today's children need these experiences more than ever, and practitioners need information about how they relate to language and literacy development, and ideas about how to integrate them into their daily routine.

Ros's sudden death was a terrible blow to everyone who knew her, but we were determined that her joyous vision of early learning would continue to influence practitioners, making children's introduction to reading and writing as enjoyable and effective as possible. I'm therefore deeply grateful to her greatest friend (and early years colleague) Lynn Broadbent, who has brought the practical activities up-to-date, advised me on the revision of my 'what' and 'why' pages, and illustrated how *Foundations of Literacy* can sit comfortably alongside England's revised EYFS.

Introduction

When Ros and I wrote the original Introduction, pointing out that over-emphasis on Early Learning Goals for literacy could lead to developmentally inappropriate practice, the EYFS hadn't been dreamed of. But a decade is a long time in politics. The EYFS framework of practice – including those Early Learning Goals – was imposed by law in 2008 on anyone looking after pre-school children outside the home. There were so many concerns about the consequent bureaucratisation and 'schoolification' of early childcare that, only four years later, the EYFS had to be revised. The literacy goals in the latest version are slightly less demanding than those required over the last ten years, but the political and educational culture which spawned them is much the same.

Primary education in England is still dominated by tests, targets, league tables and a punitive inspection regime. This culture has affected parents' attitudes and expectations, making many fear their child might be 'left behind', and increasing the pressure on practitioners (especially in Nursery and Reception classes) to over-focus on developing specific literacy skills. As well as the Early Learning Goals, practice is now likely to be distorted by the prospect of a rigorous phonics test in Year 1.

Even though the educational systems of Scotland, Wales and Northern Ireland are generally less prescriptive than that in England, parents and professionals everywhere are affected by the prevailing culture of fear, so early years practitioners across the UK are often subject to the same sorts of pressure. The very early starting age in UK schools adds to the problem. All too often, this 'toxic cocktail' leads to behaviour that caring adults know in their hearts isn't developmentally appropriate and which, increasingly, international research confirms is counter-productive.

It's no coincidence that, when UNICEF surveyed the well-being of children in the developed world, the UK came, shamefully, bottom of the league – 21st out of 21 countries surveyed. Nor that, despite frantic attempts to improve children's performance in literacy, the UK has slipped steadily down the international literacy charts (19th at the last count). In the European countries that came top for well-being (the Netherlands) and literacy (Finland), there is far greater respect for early childhood and the importance of play, while formal education doesn't start until children are at least six.

So the message of *Foundations of Literacy* is that, in terms of early learning, fun tends to be much more successful than fear. In a well-organised setting, where practitioners understand the developmental foundations on which literacy is based and provide enjoyable activities to support their development, most children are likely to achieve the relevant Early Learning Goals 'naturally' through their own emergent reading and writing activities. With plenty of attention to the seven strands of *Foundations of Literacy*, starting as soon as children begin pre-school education (see Chapter 8 for advice on the appropriate balance at different ages), most of them should also acquit themselves well in the Year 1 phonics test.

However, the children who **don't** achieve the Early Learning Goals 'naturally' are unlikely to benefit from fear-generated over-focus on specific literacy skills. They are the very children who, in the pre-school years, need a greater emphasis on communication and language, and plenty of **time** for physical, social and emotional development. *Foundations of Literacy* was devised from the start to place language, listening and literacy skills within the wider context of children's overall physical and mental growth – recognising the overlap between all areas of early learning and development, as shown in Appendix 10.

The revised EYFS is informed by developmental theory, and – if practitioners can resist the pressure to push children to 'perform' – can provide a helpful framework for early years practice. In terms of literacy, we have tried to provide here a research-based rationale for basing that practice on care rather than control, learning rather than teaching, and fun rather than fear.

Over the last decade, I've often thanked God that, in 2002, a mutual friend put me in touch with Ros Bayley. Her sheer joy for life, combined with deep understanding of the way human beings learn, taught me far more about the value of play than endless hours poring over research studies and learned tomes on child development. Lynn and I hope this new edition of Foundations of Literacy will help spread Ros's wisdom to another generation of early years practitioners.

Sue Palmer, 2013

Learning to listen

There can be little doubt that, in terms of literacy – and perhaps all school-based education – the most fundamental skill of all is *listening*. Unless children can listen, discriminatively and with growing attention, they will be slow to understand and slow to talk. As they grow older, they'll have difficulty relating and attending to their teachers, which easily leads to behavioural problems and disaffection, blighting the ability to learn throughout their school career.

For many years it's been clear to early years practitioners that – in an increasingly noise-filled world – children's listening skills are being steadily eroded. Television, DVDs, laptops, iPads and computer games now fill homes with daylong electronic noise. Shared family mealtimes, once a daily opportunity for conversational speaking and listening, have given way to screen-dominated grazing. Despite research showing that communication (and children's emotional development) is adversely affected, many parents still choose to put their children in pushchairs that face outwards, so they don't even chat to their little ones as they wheel them down the road. Gradually, scarcely noticing it has happened, our society has stopped teaching its children how to listen.

It's therefore extremely important that, as soon as possible, we make learning to listen (and its counterpart, learning to speak – see Chapter 2) a major focus of attention. For children from 'language-poor' backgrounds, with little experience of listening and being listened to, this may not be easy. It requires informed, structured attention over an extended period. We therefore need to take our lead from colleagues in Europe, who provide structured listening skills programmes, starting when children are three and continuing until they are six or seven.

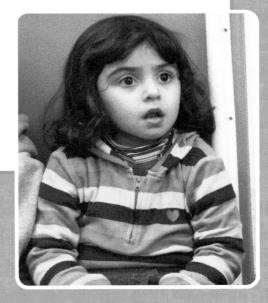

Discrimination of sounds

Many children need help in the most basic listening skill of all – discriminating a foreground sound against background noise. It's what children must learn to do in their first year of life, in order to learn language: single out their mother's voice from the irrelevant noise of their surroundings. In the past, this went without saying, but in an increasingly noisy world we can't assume it will happen naturally.

Indeed, speech and language therapist Sally Ward, who conducted a long-term study at the end of the last century, found a disturbing deterioration in babies' ability to discriminate significant sounds. In 1984, 20% of the nine-month-old infants she tested were unable to listen selectively; by 1999, the proportion had risen to 40%. In an interview in 1997, Dr Ward predicted that 'that by the early years of the new millennium, around half the nation's one-year-olds will be unable to listen satisfactorily to the sound of their mothers' voices against the noise of the television'. It's hugely important, therefore, that as soon as children arrive in a pre-school setting, we provide opportunities to help them develop this essential skill.

Once able to single out significant sounds, they can then learn to discriminate and attend to a widening range of auditory information, through plenty of musical activities, 'listening walks' and games. The ability to listen discriminatively is vital if children are to achieve the fine discrimination between speech sounds needed for clear articulation and phonological awareness (see Chapter 6).

A crucial aspect of playing listening games, such as those suggested opposite, is to increase the confidence and skills of those children who find listening particularly difficult. Children who aren't able to listen discriminatively during games need opportunities to play the game in a smaller group. Less skilled listeners also need plenty of opportunities for one-to-one interaction with an adult in a quiet environment (see page 20).

A child who is consistently baffled by the sort of activities suggested opposite may have a problem with hearing. If you are concerned, seek specialist help immediately.

Foreground sound against background noise

Dodgems

Familiarise children with a particular sound (for example clapping, tambourine, bell), which is the signal both to 'start' and 'stop'. At the 'start' signal, children pretend to be cars, speeding around (avoiding each other!), and making an appropriate noise. Make the sound again to signal 'stop', and give a few moments for all children to respond. Give praise for recognising the signal, and continue the game.

Statues

Play some lively music with a strong beat and explain to the children that they can dance to the music, but that when you shout 'stop!' over the top of the music they must freeze like statues! Go on to explain that when you shout 'go!' they can begin to dance again. If you prefer, you can use musical instruments for the 'stop!' and 'go!' signals!

Traffic Lights

Explain to the children that they are going to be vehicles driving along the road and that they are to respond to the traffic lights as quickly as possible! Further explain that you will shout out a colour, and that when you do they must respond with the appropriate action. So when you shout 'amber' they are to bend down and touch the floor, when you shout 'red' they must stop and stay completely still, and when you shout 'green,' they can begin to move again. They particularly enjoy this game if you give out paper plates for them to use as steering wheels!

Widening the range of aural discrimination

Listening walks

Take children on a walk around the school building or grounds, or out in the local area. Explain that you are going to listen for any sounds, such as cars, birds, people talking, and so on. Tell the children they have to keep very quiet and if they hear a sound they must put up a hand, whereupon everyone must stop. Invite the child to say what sound it was. Progress may be slow but once they get good at this get them to stop every so often instead and 'collect' the sounds they have heard. You can integrate a 'listening section' into any outing.

Spot the Sound

Choose a number of items with recognisable sounds, for example a music box, a ticking clock, an automatic timer, or sounds recorded on tape. Gather the children together and explain that, while they close their eyes, you are going to hide a 'sound' somewhere in the classroom. On your signal they have to listen hard and guess (a) what it is and (b) where it's hidden.

Who is it?

Sit one child on a chair with their back to the rest of the children. Explain to the children that if you tap them on the head they are to say, 'Who is it?' The child on the chair attempts to identify the voices of the children as they ask the question. Whenever they play the game they can try to break their own record.

Games on tape

There are many commercially available games using taped sounds for use in free time, for example Sound Lotto activities (see Recommended resources page 135). It is also fun to make your own, using sounds familiar to the children, especially snippets of their own voices for them to guess who's who.

Social listening

Circle time is an opportunity to model attentive listening. In the early stages keep the circles small (four to five children). As they build up the capacity to attend, gradually build the size of the circle in which they participate.

Listening in one-to-one conversation involves making frequent eye contact with the speaker. In a group situation – such as when a practitioner is talking to a number of children – eye contact is even more important, as it signals to the speaker that the listeners are attending to his/her words. Young children with poor language skills particularly need to attend to the speaker's facial expression and gestures, as these provide support for the spoken words.

However, many children these days find it difficult to make eye contact, perhaps because in homes where screen-based entertainment is a constant presence, people look at the screens rather than each other. The ability to look someone in the eye should therefore be developed as early as possible.

Other specific social skills include:

- **attending to the speaker (for example focusing, not fidgeting, ignoring distractions – gradually building up attention span)**

- **remembering and responding to what is said**

- **turn-taking.**

While it's easy and natural for children to focus attention when they are emotionally engaged, they must also learn to follow social conventions in less interesting contexts! This involves awareness of what is required and opportunities to practise behaviour in non-threatening, pleasurable circumstances.

For instance, young children, who are still developing their sense of balance, often find it difficult to sit still if their bodies are unsupported. During activities that require careful listening (such as circle time), they'll concentrate better if seated on chairs with back support. It's also important to ensure the content of 'social listening' tasks doesn't overload their auditory memory – they need gradually to build up their listening capacity over time. And, where specific responses are required, children also need thinking time (see page 21) in order to process the content and work out what they're going to say.

Learning to listen also involves seeing plenty of models of acceptable behaviour – and that means you! In class and group discussion, and when talking with children individually, it's important to demonstrate how a good listener behaves. In a busy classroom this isn't always easy, so efficient organisational and management techniques are extremely important (see page 12).

See also Social language skills – page 34

Activities

Here's looking at you, kid

Teach children how to make eye contact by using it as a selection device – for instance, when it's time to go and get their coats to go home. So, for example say, *I'm not going to say your name when it's time to get your coat today, I'm going to look at you*. This is usually guaranteed to ensure all eyes are fixed on yours, dying to make contact! Once they're familiar with this technique, choose individual children to be today's 'looker'.

Circle time

Many circle time activities encourage eye contact and turn-taking, from 'passing a look (or a wink) around the circle' to games like those below. Details of many circle time resources for early years are given on pages 135-136.

Welcome!

Make children want to look and listen to you with daily compliments! As they arrive in school, have an adult 'greeter', whose job is to look each new arrival in the eye and say something positive, such as *I love your hairband today!*, *What a happy smiling face – you brighten my day!*, *That's a gorgeous red jumper. Is it new?*

Encourage children to respond if they wish.

Signal!

You need: a favourite soft toy and a bell, whistle or musical instrument.

Sit the children in a circle and explain that the toy is going to be taken for a ride around the circle. When the bell rings, whoever's holding the toy must stop as quickly as possible and hold it perfectly still.

As the toy is passed round the children should follow it around the circle with their eyes. As they get better at responding to the signal, increase the challenge by asking them to pass the toy in the opposite direction when the bell rings. Or instead of using a sound, have them watch your face and stop passing the toy when you wink!

Mystery object

You need: a mystery object, for example a toy car or a piece of Lego.

Put the mystery object into an envelope. Explain you will whisper in the ear of the child next to you, telling them what's in the envelope. They must then whisper to the next child, and so on around the circle. When everyone's had a turn, open the envelope – have they named the object correctly?

Toys go for a spin

You need: soft toys and musical instruments.

Explain that the children, in a circle, are going to pass one of the toys around until there is a signal. Agree with the children what the signals will mean, for example the whistle means they must carry the toy to the person directly opposite them; the tambourine means give the toy to a boy; the shaker – give it to a girl. Let them suggest what should happen on the signals. As they become more skilled, try having more than one toy moving around at once.

Developing aural attention span

Listening games and activities should be pitched at the gradual and incremental development of children's aural attention span. For children whose early life has been filled with screen-based visual stimuli – and who are also used to being able to 'rewind' at will if they don't catch something first time – this is not always easily achieved. However, it's well worth the effort. An OfSTED report on the education of six-year-olds in Finland, Denmark and England noted that children in the Scandinavian countries – where listening is targeted in this way from the age of three – were more attentive, concentrated for longer, and had a higher boredom threshold than English children. They were also considerably better behaved. One important element in encouraging children to listen is to ensure that what you have to say is worth listening to! Over-exposure of your voice for behaviour management or organisation can lead some children to switch off. Look for ways of substituting other modes of communication wherever possible, for instance:

- **instead of using your voice to attract children's attention, devise a physical signal such as holding one arm in the air, and ask children to respond by quietly signalling back**

- **if there are routines or rules you frequently need to repeat, make a picture poster of them that you can just point to (symbols such as Picture Communication System are available commercially (see page 135) or use a simple tune (played on a percussion instrument) or a song (see page 43) as the signal for a particular activity**

- **for children who constantly need reminding how to behave in a group situation, make visual cue cards that you or another adult can hold up**

- **provide a daily timetable with visual cues for each element of each particular session, so children can refer to it when they come in, and throughout the day – then they always know what to expect.**

Once children have developed a reasonable level of attention, it also helps to use audio resources, such as poems, songs and short stories. These bring other voices into the classroom and provide a powerful motivation to listen carefully first time around – especially if you provide a focus by suggesting something they are to listen for.

Children who, despite a carefully planned course of listening activities, are still unable to concentrate may have Attention Deficit Disorder, and should be referred to an educational psychologist for assessment. However, while there is no doubt that this condition exists, we believe many children have been falsely diagnosed in the past simply because of poorly developed listening skills and/or too few opportunities for active outdoor play.

Activities

The spinning bottle

You need: a plastic bottle.

Sit a small group of children in a circle and explain that you are going to spin the bottle and then shout out someone's name. Go on to explain that the person whose name is called has got to try and pick up the bottle before it stops spinning. Call the children's names at random until everyone has had a go.

Toss the beanbag

You need: a beanbag for each child and a bowl, bucket or hoop.

Sit the children in a circle with the bowl, bucket or hoop in the middle. Give out the beanbags and explain that on a given signal they are to toss their beanbag into the receptacle in the middle of the circle. Explain that they will need to listen really carefully for their signal. (This could be their name or a number you have given them). Call out the names or numbers at random until all the beanbags have been thrown into the container. Talk through the skills and behaviours that are needed in order for the group to accomplish the task.

Quick responses

You need: three different musical instruments.

The object of this game is for the children to execute a different movement to the sound of each of the musical instruments. Negotiate how they will move to each signal, for example, jump up and down when you hear the tambourine, stamp your feet when you hear the drum and clap your hands when you hear the whistle.

Sausages

Choose one of the children's favourite storybooks and select a word that appears with reasonable frequency such as the name of the main character. Explain to the children that you are going to read the story and that they must listen very carefully for your chosen word. Further explain that each time they hear it they are to shout 'sausages!' Once they have got the hang of it, select another word and encourage the children to generate ideas for what they will shout when they hear it.

sausages!

Activities contd.

Jack in a box

Ask the children if they know what a 'Jack in a box' is, and talk about why it is called that. Explain that you are going to play a game where everyone is a 'Jack in a box'. Get the children to curl up small and tell them that they can't explode out of the box until you lift the lid. (You can do this by calling the children's names at random). Further explain that once they have 'exploded' they must try to remain completely still and quiet until all the other children have come out of their boxes. If anyone is finding the task really difficult get the children to generate ideas for how they could help this person to remain still!

Music and stories

The suggestions in Chapter 3 *Music, movement and memory* and Chapter 4 *Storytime!* provide many more opportunities for developing attention span.

Shooting stars

You need: a cut-out cardboard star for each child with either a number or picture in the middle.

Sit the children on chairs in a circle and make sure that there is one spare chair. Give out the stars and explain to the children that they have to listen very carefully for their number or picture to be called. Tell them that as soon as they hear their number or picture called out they are to move to the spare chair as quickly as possible. The next person to be called moves to the chair that they have vacated. Carry on until everyone has changed seats. Talk with the children about the behaviour and skills that are involved in carrying out this game quickly and effectively.

Worth a thought...

Do we sometimes inadvertently contribute to poor attention? A teaching assistant recently reported this conversation with a child with 'attention deficit' for whom she had responsibility:

TA: *Why do you never listen to what Mrs Williams [the teacher] says?*

Child: *There's no point. You'll tell me later anyway.*

Developing auditory memory

While developing aural attention span helps children to attend and concentrate, developing auditory memory helps them to learn. At all stages, but particularly in the early years, auditory memory seems to be bound up with kinaesthetic learning – and among the first sequences of sound children learn are rhythmic chants. We have therefore devoted an entire chapter to *Music, movement and memory*, and the suggestions here should be read alongside Chapter 3. From as early as possible, attention should be paid to helping children keep a steady beat, and every opportunity should be taken to use action rhymes and songs as a medium for learning.

Auditory memory may be employed on a short- or long-term basis. For instance, on a day-to-day basis we need short-term auditory memory to hold a phone number in mind long enough to dial it; we need long-term auditory memory for immediate recall of our own phone number, address, date of birth and so on. The games and activities provided on the following pages are mostly about developing the short-term memory skills underpinning verbal comprehension, phonetic analysis of words and other elementary aspects of literacy.

However, children also need opportunities to develop long-term auditory memory skills. Learning songs and rhymes by heart is therefore an important part of early childhood education, and once children have reached a level of language development appropriate for a three-year-old (see Appendix 1), we should be aiming to help them learn at least one new rhyme a week. In addition Chapter 4 suggests ways of helping children to internalise written language patterns through learning by heart during frequent and regular storytime activities.

Watch out for children whose general listening skills (i.e. those covered on previous pages) seem to develop satisfactorily, but who have trouble with short-term auditory memory activities. This may be an indicator of specific learning difficulties. Children should be referred to the Special Educational Needs Coordinator for dyslexia screening.

Activities

Holiday!

You need: some pictures of different modes of transport.

Sit the children in a circle with the picture cards face down in the middle of the circle. Explain to the children that you are going to pass an object around the circle and that when you shout 'stop,' or blow the whistle, the person holding the object is to choose a picture card and say, '*when I went on holiday I went by... (names vehicle)*'. The child hands the picture card to you. They then carry on passing the object around again and a second card is selected. The children repeat, '*when I went on my holiday I went by... (names vehicle), and.... (names vehicle)*'. Continue and see how many vehicles the children can recall.

Ted's walk

Make up a short story about Ted (or another favourite soft toy) going for a walk. Start off by setting the scene, for example 'One bright sunny day Ted decided to go for a walk. He walked down the road towards the shops and the first thing he saw was...' Each child chooses one thing that Ted saw. When everyone has had a turn see how many things the children can recall.

Movement directions

The children suggest different ways in which they could move and then you choose some of their ideas and give movement directions, firstly one at a time, then two at a time and them three at a time and so on. For example, jump, touch the floor and then sit down. The children experiment to see how many instructions they can remember.

The mystery bag

You need: a feely bag and an interesting object to place inside it.

Tell the children that they are to guess what is inside the feely bag and give them several alternatives. Pass the bag around the circle so that each child can make a guess from the alternatives given. When everyone has had their turn ask the chillden to recall who guessed what and who guessed the same as them. The mystery object can then be identified!

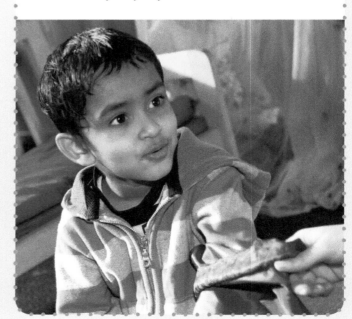

Long Tall Sally

Say the following rap, and each time you say it add one more thing until the children cannot remember any more:

When Long Tall Sally was walking down the alley well who do you think she saw?

When Long Tall Sally was walking down the alley well this is who she saw...

The children generate ideas for who Sally saw, and then repeat the rhyme, adding one more thing each time.

The shopping bag

You need: a shopping basket and a variety of objects.

Sit the children in a circle and place the objects in the middle. The children take it in turns to select an item of shopping to place into the basket. As each object is placed in the bag recite together: *We went shopping and we bought....* Continue until the children cannot remember any more. Play this game at regular intervals and encourage them to work together to beat their own record.

Sounds in sequence

You need: two sets of small instruments (for example drum, rattle, triangle, shaker, chime bar) and a screen – or ideally a puppet theatre with curtains.

Keep one set of instruments behind the screen and play two of them or, as the children become more accomplished, three, four or five in sequence. Place the instruments down in sequence, and remove any unused instruments. Place a full set of instruments in front of the screen and ask individual children to identify the instruments played and place them in sequence. Then remove the screen. When the screen is removed, the children will have immediate feedback about the accuracy of their choice. Talk about any wrong choices and why they might have happened. Gradually establish a culture of confidence in responding and lack of fear or shame about being perceived as 'wrong'.

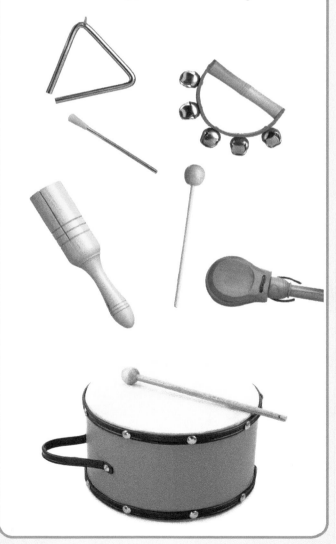

Supporting children's listening

The activities suggested on the previous pages are merely a beginning. If children are really to become active listeners, we must help them use these listening skills in their own child-initiated activities. We have to set up a 'listening culture' within which children can grow and develop as effective listeners.

- **Be a good listener.** Young children learn by listening, watching and copying, so we must be good role models! Listening is an active process requiring our full participation, and when children experience the power of being listened to, they learn by example. What we do is much more important than what we say, and as we interact with children throughout the daily routine, we must take advantage of the many opportunities that arise to demonstrate the behaviours of a good listener.

- **Be aware of what good listening involves.** Many practitioners are very supportive of children's listening, but because they do it intuitively, are not really aware of what works best and why. If we take time to reflect on what seems to work and what doesn't we can use this awareness to inform our listening in the future.

- **Be a genuine listener.** When children are playing, we need to involve ourselves sensitively in their play and listen really carefully to the things they have to say. It is not enough simply to look interested, we need to be interested in the things that are important to them, engaging them in conversations about their projects, their interests, their families and their communities. We need to consult about what's important to them and take their opinions into serious consideration. By doing this, we show them how a good, interested listener behaves.

- **Demonstrate the value of listening.** As adults, we can help children see that good listeners achieve in ways that aren't available to people who don't know how to listen. When children are involved in conflicts over space, friends or resources, we can help them listen to each other and resolve their difficulties, thus developing essential skills for life and learning.

- **Help children make links.** During periods of child-initiated learning, we can sensitively remind children of the skills they have been developing at group times and to help them to use these skills as and when appropriate. Where possible, the resources that have been used for the games and activities should be available during periods of child-initiated learning, so that children can consolidate their skills and practise and build on what they have already learned.

- **Provide a suitable environment.** Are there quiet places where children can go to listen to each other, listen to stories and play musical instruments? If we provide enough open-ended materials (for example wooden frames and plenty of drapes) the children can create dens and little secret areas where attentive listening can take place. If at all possible we should also provide a performance area where children can perform for each other and learn how to be a respectful member of an audience. If it is not possible to do so inside, space for such a purpose can usually be found outside!

Good listening does not happen by accident. It is a learnable skill, and with a consistent approach we can help all children become better listeners.

Time to talk

Speech matters: we need it to communicate and co-exist with others, to explore and express our experiences, to proclaim our needs, hopes, fears and passions. We need it to think and learn – not least to learn the skills of literacy. 'Reading and writing', said educationist James Britton, 'float on a sea of talk'.

How worrying then, that over the last quarter century many children's facility with spoken language has steadily declined. The social and environmental factors mentioned in the last chapter (television, computers, the decline of family mealtimes) have all played a part – but there are many other contributory factors. Fewer extended families, changes in working patterns, even the advent of central heating – which means that families no longer need to huddle in the same room for warmth! – have resulted in adults spending less time than ever before with their children. And this means less of the interactive language which children need to develop speech.

It's even more worrying that, while children's speaking and listening skills waned, attention to these skills in early years settings was also eroded. In England, many practitioners found the emphasis on tests, targets, and pencil-and-paper work in Key Stage 1 had a knock-on effect into Reception and pre-school provision (and, despite apparently less formal regimes, this has often also been the case in Scotland, Wales and Northern Ireland). Children have been expected to read and write earlier and earlier, and the time for developing oral language – like the time for play – has grown ever smaller.

In recent years, the proliferation of screen-based technology in early years settings (including individual hand-held devices) has further eroded opportunities for real-life, face-to-face interaction. Children need shared, multi-sensory, three-dimensional experiences in which to embed their talk. If they become hooked on screens at an early age they may develop problems with social aspects of communication, such as interpreting facial expression, body language, tone of voice and the significance of real-life, real-time context.

Thus, despite many national and local initiatives to improve children's speaking and listening skills, the prevailing culture of UK education has worked against them, with knock-on effects on many children's long-term potential for success at school. It's therefore up to practitioners to make the development of spoken language one of the highest priorities of pre-school education. As well as resisting pressure to introduce pencil-and-paper work or screen-mediated learning, this means taking every opportunity to support the development of oral language skills. This chapter offers some starting points.

Compensating for language delay

There is a well-established developmental model for language acquisition: listen, imitate, innovate, invent. Children are 'programmed' to learn naturally – given enough examples of interactive language on which to base their learning. Sadly, for many children this is not always the case at home.

Another worrying factor is researchers finding that, as children's language skills have deteriorated, practitioners' expectations have also decreased. 'Normal' language development, as defined 30 years ago, is outlined in Appendix 1. We should start with the expectation that all children can achieve these levels of speech, and give concerted help to those who start from a lower baseline.

All young children benefit when practitioners genuinely value oral learning (including its part in children's play), resisting pressure to crack on with pencil-and-paper activities. In such an environment, children with language delay are much more likely to catch up with their peers. However, they also need opportunities for one-to-one talk with adults, preferably involving a daily 'focused talk' session. One way to tackle this is to give each adult a list of up to six of the most needy children, with each of whom they arrange to spend five or ten minutes each day targeting language development. Adults can then

just pick up on what's happening naturally in the setting, addressing children's language in context and at the appropriate level.

Talk during child-initiated activities is often particularly productive, as the more contextualised language is, the easier it is to learn. When cooking, playing, making something or engaged in role-play, children can use all their senses to support new vocabulary or language structures. However, you have to be very careful and sensitive when intervening in this way – see the next page.

In addition, of course, we need to ensure that all opportunities for talk with all children are exploited as productively as possible and to include regular group 'talk time' sessions throughout the day.

> Given focused attention within an overall structured language curriculum, many children with language delay make rapid progress. Those who don't should be referred to a speech therapist for assessment. They may well benefit from small group work using a programme such as Spirals – see page 135.

Expand sentences

This mirrors the way parents initially introduce language to their children – by picking up on what the child says, and expanding on it, for example

Child: *Daddy gone.*

Adult: *Yes. Daddy's gone home.*

When expanding a sentence, take care not to expand it too much – just enough to give the child an achievable model.

Provide alternatives

If you're not sure what the child means, try to provide simple alternatives, for example

Child: *Doggy naughty goed out.*

Adult: *Oh, the doggy was naughty, was he? Did he run away? Or did mummy send him out?*

Again, try to keep the language you use simple enough for the child to pick up in a reply and avoid offering yes/no or single word replies. Ideally, you want the child to have to answer in a longer sentence, picking up on the language you have provided.

Model 'pole-bridging' talk

Pole-bridging talk is the sort of running commentary young children often use to accompany their actions (see also page 22). Rather than asking the child *What are you doing?* sit alongside and comment: *I see you're playing in the sand. I think I'll play too – I'm making a castle. I have to heap up the sand like this...* providing plenty of silences for child to respond/join in if they want to. Pitch your talk at an appropriate level for the child – i.e. short clear sentences and plenty of simple nouns and verbs. As well as providing clear language models, this approach has the advantage that it often encourages children to start speaking themselves, picking up on the structures and vocabulary you have provided.

Give plenty of time

Ask questions sparingly (see page 24) but when you do – or when you ask oblique questions (for example *I wonder what that's called?*) give plenty of time for the child to answer. Count up to 15 in your head, and then, if appropriate, offer to say it again. Waiting for a response can feel strange, and adults often feel embarrassed for the child, but many children do need plenty of processing time. You may have to tackle this issue with the other children too. For instance, if a child with language delay is taking a long time to respond during circle time, and the others are beginning to get restive, explain: *Sometimes we all need some extra thinking time. In our circle, we wait politely for people to think what they want to say. And it helps if we stay quiet too.*

Offer visual support

Children with language delay often find visual support particularly helpful – so whenever possible support what you're saying with pictures, photographs and actual artefacts that they can hold. In fact, this technique helps all children, including those speaking English as an additional language. Some children also find symbols helpful, especially for more abstract words. These can be either pictorial symbols, such as PCS (see Resources, page 135), or physical signs, such as those in British Sign Language.

Use puppets and soft toys

Puppets and soft toys add excitement and engagement to learning activities for all children, but can be especially useful with shy children and those with language delay. A child who finds talking to adults difficult will often 'open up' to a puppet or soft toy.

Talk during child-initiated learning

Talk during child-initiated activities helps children absorb new vocabulary and language structures easily, as there is a direct, concrete link between what they are doing and what you are saying. A self-chosen activity is also likely to be a motivating one for the child, which again makes learning more productive. Practitioners should therefore take every opportunity to engage all children in talk during periods of child-initiated learning.

However, while sensitive interaction with children at play is one of the most important skills of the early years practitioner, it is also one of the most subtle. Most of us, anxious to extend children's learning, have gone rushing into a play situation, only to find that the children have all got up and walked away! When approaching a child or children with a view to talk:

- stand back and look carefully at what is going on

- tune into what they are saying and/or doing, then quietly sit down and begin to play with some of the materials and equipment they are using

- once they're comfortable with your presence, engage in some 'self-talk' (see 'pole-bridging talk' opposite) describing what you are doing – talking to yourself rather than directly addressing the child

- usually, within a short space of time children will begin to respond to your self-talk, and once this has happened you can begin to extend both their play and their language.

Pole-bridging talk

It is natural for young children to talk to themselves as they do or make something, giving a sort of running commentary on their activity. Sometimes known as 'pole-bridging talk', this is an important element in cognitive development (Vygotsky suggests that the 'exterior monologue' of pole-bridging talk becomes an 'interior monologue', which is then automatised as thought). For children from 'language poor' backgrounds, however, pole-bridging talk is often impoverished, with lots of vague words (for example *It go brmm*) instead of more precise nouns and verbs (for example *The racing car's starting up and now it's steaming down the track, brmm!*). It therefore helps to model pole-bridging talk, thus providing children with vocabulary within a very meaningful context (see pages 23-24).

Activities

Follow the children's lead

Follow children's leads and take turns with them. When they are deeply engaged in activities, children usually have a clear sense of purpose and a well defined pattern of thinking. It is when adults tap into this that the most productive talk takes place. Any attempt to introduce another agenda can only result in frustration and lost opportunities.

Be conversational

Use their comments as conversational openers: listen carefully to children and repeat back what they say. This gives value to what they have said and encourages them to keep talking, for example

Child: *This car go fast...fast...very fast.*

Adult: *This car goes very, very fast.*

Child: *That 'cause it racing car.*

Adult: *That's because it's a racing car. Would you like to drive a racing car?*

Seek enlightenment

One type of questioning that is often successful, however, is a display of 'genuine' curiosity. Rather than asking questions like a teacher, ask them like an equal – for instance, asking children how they did something or asking for their help. This less direct, social questioning shows that you are interested in and respect their ideas, and can also help move their ideas on.

Expand and extend

Expand and extend on what the children are doing. This can be thought of as a natural conversation technique where the adult introduces new ideas into the discussion in order to develop new ideas and vocabulary, for example

Child: *When I went to the fair I went on the waltzers and it was great.*

Adult: *I went on the waltzers once, but I didn't like it.*

Child: *Why not, why didn't you like it?*

Adult: *It made me dizzy.*

Child: *Why did it do that?* (You now have an opening to introduce new ideas and vocabulary.)

Activities contd.

Model pole-bridging talk

This is one of the most valuable things we can do to develop both language and cognitive development, and it's very easy once you've practised a few times. There are many occasions when it is appropriate:

- during any play (indoor and out) and role-play

- when you or a child are making something or engaged in any creative activity.

There are two ways you can use the technique:

- Pole-bridge on behalf of the child or children you are sitting with. Describe their actions, thus providing them with the relevant vocabulary, for example *You are putting all of the dinosaurs in the bucket!*

- Pole-bridge on behalf of yourself. Describe your own actions as you do something sitting alongside a child, for example *I think I'll make a necklace. I'm going to thread this piece of macaroni on to the string. I'll have to push it through the hole there. Now I'm pulling it along...*

But remember to leave plenty of long gaps between sections of your commentary, so that the child can join in or take over. If the child is clearly irritated by your presence, stop!

Avoid the Spanish inquisition

Ask questions sparingly. Questions can put children on the spot and if they don't know the answer – or if they don't have the vocabulary or facility with language to answer – they often just freeze up. Tentative language can often be more effective, for example *I wonder why the sand did that...*

Vocabulary development

Selected words and phrases related to topic work, storytime or other activities should be actively targeted each week, from Nursery through to Year 1. Each week, these should include words that:

- name, for example postman, elephant

- denote actions, for example bring, carry

- describe, for example friendly, huge, gently

- categorise, for example jobs, animals (and words that fall in the categories)

- denote position, for example in, under, behind, between

- denote sequence, for example when, after

- are used for reasoning, for example if, but, because, so.

It helps to make a poster of current target words, so that all adults in the setting are constantly reminded of them and make an effort to bring them into general conversation.

It can take many exposures to a new word before children become confident in using it themselves – although the more motivating and meaningful the context, the more likely they are to acquire new vocabulary quickly. It's therefore important to ensure that, as well as the specific 'teaching context', there are other opportunities (for example appropriate role-play area, dressing-up clothes, small world, games, stories) in which the target words can crop up. Adults can then engage in pole-bridging talk (see pages 22-24) alongside children, and encourage children to pole-bridge too – or use the vocabulary naturally in role-play conversation.

Keep a record of words you have targeted, and return to them occasionally. Some children need to keep revisiting familiar words and expressions to gain in language confidence.

All children misuse words occasionally, but watch out for children who seem excessively confused about vocabulary items. This may indicate an underlying language disorder, and the child should be referred to a speech and language therapist for assessment.

Words that name

What's in the bag?

You need: an attractive bag and a collection of interesting objects.

Sit the children in a circle with the objects in the middle. Pass the bag around the circle. When you shout 'stop,' the child holding the bag chooses an object from the collection. Encourage them to say, '*I am putting a ....into the bag.*' (You can vary the objects according to the vocabulary you wish to focus on.) When several people have had a turn, try to recall who put what into the bag.

Words that describe

Feely bag

You need: a feely bag of items of different sizes, shapes, textures, colours.

Children take turns to come out and feel for an item, which they then get to look at, while keeping it hidden from the rest of the class. The child then describes the item, for others to guess. Model this process a few times and, if necessary, give children cues (see Report activity on page 33).

Words denoting position

An obstacle course!

Set up an obstacle course in the outside area and as children enjoy negotiating their way through, label and describe their actions. Then encourage them to chorus what they're doing as they move (Under the chair, over the bench, through the hoop, etc.).

Rosie's Walk

Read the story of *Rosie's Walk* by Pat Hutchins, then make your own book featuring positional language. Photograph the children under the table, on top of the climbing frame, going through the gate etc. When they are the main characters in a book they are infinitely interested in it!

Words that denote actions

What am I doing?

Ensure everyone can see everyone else, then perform a simple mime, for example washing face, eating a banana, brushing teeth. Encourage everyone to copy your mime and name what you're doing. Let the children take turns to start the mime. If they cannot think of actions, use picture cards as a prompt.

How shall we move?

Everyone moves around the room mingling with each other until you give the signal to stop. You then point to someone and ask them to choose a way for the group to move, for example jumping, flying, hopping, swooping etc. When you signal again, everyone stops and another child chooses how to move. You may need to model this process a few times until the children get the hang of it.

Words that categorise

Where does it belong?

One of the most effective ways to encourage children to classify objects is to make sure that everything in your setting is well labelled and that there is a place for everything. This provides the children with naturally occurring opportunities to sort and classify when they are getting things out and putting them away again.

Burglar Bill

You need: a sack and collection of objects from around the classroom.

Tell the children that you found the sack of objects outside the classroom. (Invite them to offer their ideas for how it got there!). Empty the bag into the middle of the circle, explaining that all the things will need to he sorted out. Hoops are good for sorting into. Model how to choose an item and sort it into the appropriate category, for example *I am going to put this spade over here because it belongs with the sand toys.* The children take turns to classify the remaining objects.

Words denoting sequence

Washing line stories

Peg four pictures, cut-outs or even objects along a washing line, and invent a story in which four events happen in sequence, for example a character goes for a walk and finds or does things. Model how to tell the story using First... next... then... (you could also add in the end... as a way of winding up the story.) Ask children to tell their own stories, using their own washing line items if they wish. Later add in more sequential words, for example later, finally, after that...

Words used for reasoning

These words are used naturally whenever language is used to explore, analyze or explain (see pages 31-33).

Repetition and innovation

Children learn to talk by imitating the language of adults, then innovating on these language structures to make them their own. We can help build children's command of vocabulary, sentence structures and questioning techniques through providing language models for them to repeat. This sounds rather dreary, but if transformed into games and role-play can be great fun. Songs (see Chapter 3) and storytime (see Chapter 4) also provide many opportunities for children to imitate the language structures they hear.

When children join in with a song, chant along with a rhyme or chorus responses in a game, those with poor auditory memory are carried along by their more fortunate peers. Even if they're not word perfect, they become steadily more familiar with the rhythms and patterns of language, picking up vocabulary as they go. And even though they're 'learning by rote', the words eventually lodge in their brains – with sufficient support from context-based activity, the concepts will follow (this is why generations of children found chanting the times

tables at primary school helped with maths later in their school careers). Although it's traditional in the UK to frown on 'rote learning', practitioners in Europe have always recognised its value in developing oral and aural language skills.

Once a particular language structure is familiar, children can be asked to innovate on it. A powerful vehicle for this is circle time – many excellent resources are listed on page 135. A typical circle time activity is to provide a frame, such as *My favourite place is ... because ...* , for each child to complete. If the circle consists of eight children and an adult, by the end of the activity everyone has heard that particular language construction nine times. If the next frame is *I don't like going to ... because ...* , that's another nine exposures to the same basic 'reason-giving' structure. And all in the name of Personal, Social and Emotional Development! Incidentally, don't worry if some children occasionally 'copy' the responses of others – they're still practising language, and gaining in confidence in a social skill.

Activities

Mr Copycat

You need: a puppet or soft toy to be 'Mr Copycat'.

Introduce the toy to the children, and explain that whatever he says, you want them to repeat. You may ask them to do it in chorus to start with, then ask individuals. Mr Copycat (with you as ventriloquist) can then provide sentences that are just at the edge of challenge for the children. Once they've got the idea, vary the activity by asking them to repeat the sentence in a very quiet voice, a loud voice, a robot voice, and so on.

The toy shop

You need: pictures of toys cut from a catalogue (provide several of each one to avoid disappointment).

Sit the children in a circle with the pictures in the middle. Explain the children are going to pretend they are visiting the toy shop and can choose any toy they'd like. Model the language, e.g. *My name is... and I am choosing a...* Support children who need it by putting in the language for them – with practice, they'll soon be joining in.

Try the game with colours, fruit or sweets. You can vary it to accommodate the vocabulary you wish to teach.

Raps and rhymes

These are a great way of encouraging repetition and innovation, and when language is framed in a rap it also becomes much easier to remember.

What will you play today?

What will you play with today (insert child's name)?
What will you play with today?
What will you play with today? (name)
Are you ready to say?

Child answers: *Today I'm going to play with...*

The monkey in town

As I was walking through the town I saw a monkey bending down.
He was bending down and looking at the ground ...
and this is what he found ...

The children then repeat the rhyme, and each time they repeat it they have the monkey find something different.

Activities contd.

Pass the parcel

You need: interesting objects, one of which is duplicated and wrapped in a parcel.

Sit the children in a circle with the objects in the middle. Explain that one of the objects is the same as the one in the parcel. As the parcel is passed around the circle they can guess what's inside. Model the language they need, e.g. *I think that there is a ... inside the parcel*. Children having difficulties can pick up the object while you model the language for them. As the parcel goes around the children will hear the language frequently repeated. As children become more skilled they can give a reason for their choice. Once they've all had a turn open the parcel and find out what's inside.

Snap shots

Ask the children to bring in a photograph of a member of their family. Sit them in a circle and model how the children are to introduce the person in their photograph, for example *This is my ... his/her name is ... I like them because*, etc. The children become really engaged with this activity because of the level of emotional engagement.

What's this for?

You need: a puppet, teddy or soft toy, and a collection or familiar resources.

Explain to the children that your puppet or toy is going to spend the day in your setting, but that he does not understand what all the toys are for and how they are used. Further explain that the children are going to tell him about how each thing is used.

Begin by selecting an object and modelling how to give information about it, providing as much information as appropriate for their language level, for example *This is called a ...We use it for ... You have to remember ...* The children then take it in turns to choose an object and as they pass it around the circle each child adds to the information.

Developing expressive language

When talking with young children in any context, the use of certain types of expressive language will specifically **PREPARE** them for literacy and learning. We need language to mediate thought when we: **P**lan, **R**ecount, **E**xplore, **P**redict, **A**nalyze, **R**eport and **E**xplain, but these are the types of language use which children from 'language poor' backgrounds often do not use. See the chart in Appendix 2.

The questions on the chart are not designed to be used as a bombardment! They are simply a guide to the sorts of thinking involved in using language in each of these ways. We must be wary of asking children too many questions, as they may not have the vocabulary with which to answer – or, indeed, a clear understanding of underlying concepts, which are often bound up with language. We have to build up this language and understanding gradually by:

- providing models of language use, for example through pole-bridging talk, or as part of a story

- where possible, providing activities in which these models can be used for repetition and innovation – perhaps through storytelling, drama or role-play

- introducing questioning gradually, once we've ensured children are equipped with the vocabulary and experience to answer

- helping children themselves frame questions – again, repetition and innovation can help.

It is helpful to enlarge the **PREPARE** chart and display it as a poster to act as an aide-mémoire for practitioners during adult- and child-initiated activities. In Reception and Year 1, a further poster displaying key question words – *who, what, when, where, why, how and how did you feel?* (accompanied by appropriate symbols) – helps both pupils and practitioners ensure that spoken accounts and anecdotes are as explicit as possible.

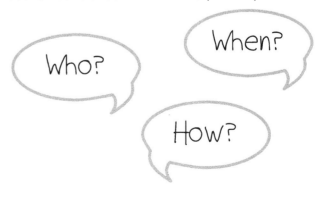

Plan

Hold planning sessions directly before periods of child-initiated learning. Talk about what children plan to do and how they'll go about it. Make use of sequencing language (*first... next ... after that...*). Encourage children to talk through their plans. Use the 'phone a friend' technique to make this more fun: have plenty of telephones available, and put the children into pairs so that they can tell their plan to each other.

Recount

At the end of a period of child-initiated learning, hold a recount session. Choose a few children to talk about what they did and what happened. (Play games to choose who'll recount next, for example describe someone, and when the children guess who it is, that person recounts; or spin a bottle and the person it is pointing to when it stops tells what they did.) Stress sequencing language for example *first... next ... after that....*

You can also target recount with children throughout the session, encouraging them to talk about what they've been doing. However, when children are deeply engaged in an activity they sometimes don't want to talk, so be sensitive to their needs.

Explore

Bring in interesting items (or collections of items) for the children to explore, for example some 'snowstorms'; locks and keys; nuts and bolts; sparkly costume jewellery.

Model exploratory talk: *I wonder what this is ... I think that bit might be for ...* When children are exploring, use pole-bridging talk to describe their actions and bring their thoughts to life: *You're giving that snowstorm a good shake. I wonder what will happen. Where did all the snow come from? I think there must be some water in there or something. The little people are still where they were before. I wonder if that one's the same.*

Leave plenty of gaps for children to join in, or take over the commentary.

Report

Create a feely bag (see *Words that describe* activity on page 26). To report using other senses, collect a variety of food items (for example piece of cheese, tomato ketchup, cocktail sausage, jam, slice of lemon, marshmallow, mashed potato). Invite children one by one behind a screen, and give an item to hold, feel, sniff and taste. As they do so ask them to describe it, for the others to guess. Model this first, and perhaps help with vocabulary such as sour, salty, etc. Go on to visual aspects, such as colour, size, shape only after exhausting the descriptive potential of the other senses.

Explain

When interesting phenomena occur or the group is looking at an item of interest, use talking partners (see page 35) to discuss 'how' and 'why' questions. When children have had a minute or two to talk it over, listen to a few explanations and let the group say which they think most likely.

Analyze

Be adventurous with water play. Freeze old keys or small world toys into blocks of ice (use margarine containers). Leave by the water tray, and join in the amazement when they're discovered. *What on earth...? What's that ice like? I wonder how it got in there? How can we get it out? Gosh, wasn't that a surprise? I felt really amazed.* Encourage the children (a) to observe through different senses and to consider what they observe (b) to talk about what they notice, what is happening, and how they feel about it. Another time fill balloons or plastic gloves with water and freeze them.

Predict

Use stories as a vehicle for prediction (see Chapter 4). As you tell or read a story, stop once in a while to discuss what might happen next. This is a good opportunity for partnered talk. When children have had a minute or so to talk with a partner, invite a few pairs to give their predictions. This can lead you into wondering *I wonder why you think that?* and to linking the prediction to what is already known.

Social language skills

In Chapter 1 Learning to listen we looked at two important elements in the social use of language: making eye contact and maintaining attention within conversation. The complementary conversational speaking skills include:

- engaging the listener's attention (i.e. awareness of and response to one's audience)

- turn-taking.

Children need models of these behaviours and opportunities to develop social language skills in context. One of the best contexts is role-play, where the adoption of a role allows the child to distance him/herself from the language to some extent, and thus learn from mistakes without personal embarrassment.

All children need frequent opportunities to talk:

- one-to-one with an adult, who can model both speaking and listening skills (this is particularly important for children with language delay - see page 20)

- one-to-one with a peer, for example a 'talking partner'(see opposite and also Chapter 4, *Storytime)*

- in a small group of peers, for example in the role-play area. The significance of role-play cannot be over-estimated as they can be skilfully adapted to provide contexts for the sort of language we want children to practise (see page 36).

- in a small group with an adult, for example circle time (see Recommended resources on page 135).

For very young children and those with language delay, small group sessions are best conducted in groups of no more than four. As children gain in confidence and competence, the group can grow in size, but small group activities involving no more than six to eight children are important throughout the early years.

- in a large group, supervised by an adult.

In the earliest stages, 'whole class' gatherings will generally be opportunities to listen rather than talk (for example early storytime activities or sing-a-longs), but as children grow in confidence, many oral activities can be conducted with the whole class.

Children on the autistic spectrum may have particular difficulties with social language skills. Consult the educational psychological services or local authority special educational needs department for further support.

Activities

Pleased to meet you

This game provides an opportunity to model a wide range of social greetings. You need a tambourine, a drum or some music. The children walk around the room changing direction as they wish until the tambourine is banged or the music stops. They then shake hands with the person nearest to them and greet each other by saying something like: *Pleased to meet you. How are you today?* Stop the music every so often to discuss possible greetings.

Turn-taking object

For children who find it difficult to take turns in conversation, try the circle time technique of using an object – a soft toy or something very special – which denotes the speaker. Only the person holding the object is allowed to talk.

Double circle

This is a way of doing circle time with a larger group, and also introducing talking partners. Invite the children to bring something from home that they would like to talk about. Bring something of your own too so you can model how to talk about an item to start them off. Make two circles of chairs, an inner circle and an outer circle, facing each other. Before the children begin to share, encourage them to think about what they want to say. Then they talk to the person sitting opposite them. If necessary, each pair can have a 'talking object' to determine who should hold the floor.

On an appointed signal they swap over, and the listener becomes the talker. When they have finished sharing, the inner circle all move round one so that the process can begin again. This enables the children to refine and build on what they want to say.

Talking partners

You can introduce talking partners through the double circle, or during conventional circle time: *Turn to the person on your left and say hello.* Provide many opportunities in this type of structured setting, for children to learn how to talk one-to-one with a peer. You could ask them on different occasions to talk about:

- favourite foods, games, animals, television programmes etc things they like doing; places they like to visit

- a time when they were excited or scared; things they think they are good at or find difficult; one person in their family; where they live; some work they have done

- what they would choose if they could have any present they wanted.

When they are used to talking to a partner, start to use the technique as a way, during large group work, of ensuring that every child gets the opportunity to talk about whatever is under discussion: *Turn to the person on your left and talk about...*

Barrier games

Social language to report:
Place a familiar object behind a screen and tell the children that you are going to describe this object without actually naming it. Tell them that their job is to listen very carefully and see if they can guess what the object is. When they have seen this modelled a few times encourage them to take on the role of the 'speaker'. Eventually, this can become a partnered task.

Social language to explain: Provide the wherewithal for making or drawing something behind the screen, for instance a Mr Potato Man. Provide identical equipment on the other side of the screen. The speaker has to create something behind the screen, while explaining what he's doing to a partner. The partner attempts to create exactly the same thing – asking questions when necessary. At the end, they compare the finished results.

Supporting talk during imaginative play

Imaginative play is extremely important for children's all-round development. It also has a crucial role to play in the development of spoken language. Research shows that when children are using the 'pretend self' in imaginative play they display much greater linguistic competence than at other times. However, if they are to gain maximum rewards from this exciting form of play, it is essential that practitioners think carefully about what is provided.

Providing the environment

Children will play imaginatively just about anywhere in the setting. Whether they are playing in the sand, the water, with small world toys, inside or out, they will be constantly pretending, and in so doing, creating new worlds and confirming familiar ones. Some children's play will be firmly grounded in home and community experiences (socio-dramatic play); others will have begun to enter imagined worlds (thematic-fantasy play). We must provide an appropriate environment and materials for both these types of play:

- a well equipped home area

- themed areas where children can engage in transactional play (where goods and services are exchanged for money) and these will vary throughout the year

- prop boxes and dressing-up clothes that can be used on an ongoing basis to enable children to engage in a wide range of pretend play

- a range of open-ended materials to stimulate the imagination so children can use them in their own way

- storyboxes with props so that children can act out their favourite stories.

The role of the adult

Before setting up any imaginative play area, give careful consideration to the following questions:

- Is what we are intending within the children's experience, and if not, what can we do about it? For instance, we could take them on a visit, read stories and look at pictures or model the role-play ourselves. Once children have seen adults model the process they will be much more confident about doing it themselves. If necessary, sit the children down in front of the role-play area and let them watch the adults role-playing.

- Can we involve the children in planning and setting up the imaginative play area? (If we can, it will be a much more important place for them.)

- Do we have a programme for observing children in the imaginative play area so that we are aware of what they are talking about and what vocabulary they are using? Only by doing this can we add new materials, make suggestions and provide further experiences that will develop their language yet further.

- Are we providing a balance of adult-initiated and child-initiated activities?

- Have we given enough consideration to how we will interact with children in the imaginative play area?

- Have we made some time each day to join the children in the role-play area?

If you are unfortunate enough to be working with restricted space, make the best possible use of story boxes, prop boxes and the outside area. (See resources using storyboxes and builder's trays on page 135.)

Music, movement and memory

Music seems to be a natural form of communication with young children[1] It provides a playful, emotionally-satisfying context for all sorts of learning, a context which is associated with relaxation and fun. Since time immemorial parents have sung nursery rhymes, played clapping games and taught action songs to entertain their children, and teachers used to continue that tradition in school. Unfortunately, however, in today's world home entertainment is more likely to come in visual form, and the old songs and chants are often forgotten. In school, time for music and song has often been eroded by the demands of the National Curriculum and standardized testing.

Music, especially song, is an obvious way of developing all the important listening skills described in Chapter 1. Since most musical activities are performed in a group, they are also ideal for developing social skills of collaboration, including turn-taking and learning to sing in time with the rest of the group (see Chapter 2). Phonemic awareness – which underpins phonics – seems to depend to a large extent on the appreciation of rhythm, auditory discrimination and memory (see Chapter 6), while musical activities – from simple clapping games, through marching, action songs and dances – also help children develop gross and fine motor control, hand-eye coordination and physical confidence – all essential for handwriting (see Chapter 7).

Given the extent to which musical experience in the early years contributes to children's ability to read and write, it's important to ensure that it is a valued part of our daily practice throughout the EYFS.

Steady beat, rhythm and rhyme

On the advice of multicultural expert: Ensure children know this is a music game. At home or in a restaurant, such behaviour with chopsticks would be the height of bad manners!

Research from the USA suggests that a young child's ability to keep a steady beat is one of the best indicators of later academic success. This will come as no surprise to Early Years practitioners, as young children who are naturally able to sing and keep time often have a maturity and language competence beyond that of their peers. In the earliest stages, steady beat may well aid the development of speech, as a sense of rhythm underlies our ability to pick up the patterns of spoken phrases and sentences. As soon as possible, therefore, we should provide activities to help children feel the strong 'pulse' or beat in speech and in music.

In terms of literacy, one of the key stages of phonological awareness, outlined on page 72, is the ability to discriminate syllables – the 'beats' within a word. Appreciation of rhythm also leads children to recognize rhyming patterns which is critical for the learning of phonics. Once they have acquired this level of

phonological awareness, children seem to delight in it, and there is a strong playground culture of clapping, skipping and 'dipping' rhymes which exploit rhythm, nonsense syllables and rhymes (for example *Ee-ny, mee-ny, mi-ny, mo; Catch a ti-ger by the toe; If he holl-ers, let him go; Ee-ny, mee-ny, mi-ny, mo; I say you are IT!*).

For reading and writing, children must also be sensitive to the rhythms and patterns of written language, which are more complex and sophisticated than the language of spontaneous speech. Musical activities lay the foundations for sensitivity to the 'tunes and cadences' of written phrases, sentences and paragraphs – what Robert Louis Stevenson called 'the chime of fair words, and the stately march of the period'. It's possible that, at a later stage of education, understanding of punctuation and the ability to read with expression have their roots in enjoyable early rhythm-based activities.

Activities

Keep the beat

1. Sit the children in a circle and put on some music with a strong beat.

2. Encourage the children to:

   a. While sitting down, pat the beat on their knees using both hands.

   b. While sitting down, pat the beat alternating hands.

   c. While sitting down, stamp the beat using feet alternatively.

   d. Walk or march to the beat while standing in one place.

   e. Walk or march to the beat in a forwards, backwards or sideways direction.

Chopsticks

You need: some paper plates and some chopsticks.

1. Give out the paper plates, and using the chopsticks play a simple sequence of sounds to a steady beat on the reverse side of the plates. For example, use the sticks to hit the floor, plate, floor, plate, floor, plate etc.

2. As the children gain in confidence and skill make the sequence more complicated. For example, floor, plate, knock your sticks together, plate, floor, plate, together, plate etc.

3. Give hands-on guidance to children experiencing difficulty. This will enable them to 'feel' the beat.

4. When children become proficient, allow them to take the lead.

5. Try this activity using cheap plastic waste paper baskets turned upside down.

Rap it out

Rapping allows children to explore the musicality of language. Begin by devising simple raps and proceed to more difficult ones like the following:

My gran's cupboard

My gran has a cupboard under the stairs
And every time I look in there
I see some things that make me shout
Some things that make my eyes pop out
I see a monster, right there,
Right there under the stairs!

(The children can generate further ideas for what might be under the stairs and then rap a sequence of things. This will really develop the auditory memory!)

Who is knocking at my door?

Ten dirty dogs came knocking at my door
Rat-a-tat, rat-a-tat, knocking at my door
Ten dirty dogs came knocking at my door
Till I said, 'dirty dogs DON'T DO IT ANY MORE'
So they didn't....but then...

(Repeat the rhyme substituting, for example: mucky monkeys, grubby gorillas, cool cats, slithering snakes etc.)

Beat out a name

1. Tell the children you are going to clap out a forename, for them to guess who it is. Clap the number of syllables in the longest names (for example Victoria, Alexander). When they are guessed, ask the owners out beside you, pronouncing their names syllabically (Vic-tor-i-a).

2. Then clap a syllable for the shortest names (for example Jade, Sam), and bring those owners, once guessed, out too.

3. Clap any remaining names until everyone is with you.

4. When children are familiar with the idea of clapping their names, you can use it in day-to-day organization, for example for lining up – *If I clap your name, stand up now. Lovely – you can go and line up. Is there anyone else: listen!* until gradually everyone is hearing the beats in words.

Articulation and song

We did not comment on articulation skills in Chapter 2, despite their importance in the development of spoken language, because of constraints of space. However, a chart describing the normal development of articulation is given in Appendix 1, and practitioners should keep an ear on children's speech to ensure this is developing appropriately*. Singing helps refine young children's articulatory skills in a pleasurable way, and songs are a good way of introducing or reinforcing new vocabulary. Singing also develops control of vocal expression, introducing a range of pitches, volumes and subtleties.

The choice of songs is important. Today's children sometimes learn to sing along with pop songs at home but these have short shelf-lives, and are not shared across the generations (especially with older practitioners!) in the same way as traditional songs. If children enjoy singing them, it's fine to include them in your repertoire, but try also to include:

- nursery rhymes and chants, which are highly rhythmic, with plenty of rhyme and alliteration, and seem to be particularly suitable in terms of preparation for phonics (see Chapter 6)

- action songs, which also engage kinaesthetic memory, and can be useful for developing motor skills, hand-eye coordination and, in the case of finger-rhymes, the muscles required for adequate pencil grip (see Chapter 7)

- songs with choruses for joining in, but particularly those which require turn-taking, or give opportunities for different children to sing variations on a familiar verse structure.

*Articulation, like all language skills, depends upon a child's hearing ability, and upon adequate exposure to interactive spoken language. If, despite these conditions being met, articulation is poor and a child does not seem able to copy your 'correct models' of pronunciation, refer him or her to a speech therapist for assessment. Take great care never to inhibit children's speech by making them self-conscious about problems with articulation.

Singing with young children

First and foremost, have fun. Singing should always be an enjoyable activity – don't worry too much about the quality of the sound produced as young children are still 'finding their voice'. Young children have a limited vocal range so avoid songs that are outside this range as they will simply be unable to join in. If you are unsure about this be aware of the type of tunes they sing spontaneously while playing! Musical accompaniment isn't necessary – indeed, music from an instrument often drowns the children out and makes it difficult for them to hear their own voices. However, they will need you to sing with them, to teach them the tune and words. Don't worry if you feel your voice is not very good – the children will not judge you. You are their model and if you sing with confidence, so will they. Commercially produced tapes and CDs are also useful as they help you maintain the beat, but make sure they are pitched appropriately for the children.

A daily sing-song

A short singing session each day is much better than a long session once a week. First thing in the morning is a very good time for a sing-along session, as it tunes the children into the day (and into speaking and listening in a group) in a pleasant way, and singing together establishes a feeling of cohesion in the class. Get children to stand up when singing as this helps them to breathe more easily and produce a better sound – also they will almost certainly want to move as they sing, whether it's an action song or not! Always begin a session with a well-known and well-loved song. Introduce new songs gradually.

Songs throughout the day

Wherever possible, integrate more songs into the daily routine of the setting, for example:

* sing the register

* use a song to introduce a regular event such as storytime – when they hear you start the song, or play the tune on a CD, everyone gradually joins in and makes their way to the story corner (This rap, by music specialist Linda Caroe, works a treat: 1, 2, 3, 4, Come and sit down on the floor; 5, 6, 7, 8, Hurry up and don't be late; 1,2,3,4 Is your bottom on the floor? 5, 6, 7, 8, Are you sitting really straight?)

* make up a tidy-up song – as generations of workers have discovered, chores become much easier if accompanied by a song (Linda Caroe's tidy-up song to the tune of *The Farmer's in his Den*: It's time to tidy up, etc. Ee, i, addio, it's time to tidy up. We're tidying the paints, etc. We're tidying the chairs, etc....)

Which songs?

When they come into an early years setting many children may already have built up a repertoire of favourite songs. Ask them what they would like to sing and encourage them to teach their favourite songs to each other. There are many tapes and CDs of nursery rhymes and songs, and the imprint A&C Black of Bloomsbury Publishing produces a wide variety of song books. Look out particularly for:

* traditional action songs, for example *There Was A Princess Long Ago; In A Cottage In A Wood; Wind The Bobbin Round; Incy Wincy Spider; If You're Happy and You Know It Clap Your Hands; The Farmer's In His Den*

* traditional songs that can be acted out or turned into action rhymes, for example *Row, Row, Row Your Boat; Polly Put The Kettle On; Twinkle, Twinkle Little Star; She'll Be Coming Round The Mountain When She Comes; Strawberry Fair; Old Uncle Tom Cobleigh*

* number and cumulative songs which, when familiar, can be adapted to give different children (or groups) a short piece each to sing, with the whole group singing the main chorus, for example *Old MacDonald Had a Farm; There Were Ten In The Bed; Ten Green Bottles; Five Little Speckled Frogs; One Man Went To Mow; One, Two, Three, Four, Five, Once I Caught A Fish Alive; Green Grow The Rushes-O!* (as children's voices extend their range).

Once children know a song well, encourage them to be innovative by playing with and changing some of the words and ideas, for example Old MacDonald could have a shop instead of a farm. Everyone could go around the roundabout instead of the Mulberry Bush.

Music and auditory memory

As we pointed out in Chapter 1, auditory memory – the ability to recall sequences of sound – is extremely important for learning, and especially for literacy learning. All musical activities involve remembering sequences of sound, and the memorization is made easier by the elements of melody, rhythm and repetition. According to evolutionary biologists, our internal programming for song is deeper than that for speech – indeed, if you want someone to remember something, put it to music (as the success of advertising jingles demonstrates). Hence the success of songs for counting, learning the alphabet, days of the week and so on.

Action songs and rhymes, marching, clapping chants and simple dances also involve the kinaesthetic learning channel, offering support for children who need extra help in developing auditory memory. Even those children who aren't yet ready to join in are still able to participate by making the movements and building up a predictive sequence in the brain. And, of course, these activities can be repeated time and again, without ever boring the children.

For activities involving a dynamic combination of music or rhythm and movement children need space – preferably much more space than is available in the average classroom. It's therefore essential that, somehow, regular provision is also made for these activities in open areas – indoors in a hall, gym or other large space, or outdoors in the play area, a park or sports field. Not only does moving to music improve auditory memory, it also helps children develop control of balance, awareness of their bodies in space, and large-scale motor movement (see Chapter 7).

The following examples illustrate how a single action rhyme or song can be useful in a variety of ways. Teach the rhyme for fun, and as a way of remembering the days of the week, colours, etc. Later, when alerting children to the long vowel sounds, revisit the familiar rhyme and ask them to listen for, then exaggerate the pronunciation of, the particular phoneme each time it occurs.

Days of the week
(and the long ay sound)

Devise suitable actions for each vehicle... end up with everyone walking round.

Monday, a plane to fly far away
Tuesday, a scooter to go out to play
Wednesday, a ship, we're sailing to Spain
Thursday, chuff chuff, we're off on the train
Friday, a rocket to blast into space
Saturday, we're in a car in a race...
Sunday, we sit and we play and we talk
Then when we're ready we'll go for a walk!

Parts of the body
(and the long ee sound)

Easy peasy lemon squeezy
Easy peasy lemon squeezy
Stretch your arms and bend your kneezy!
Rub your tum and bend your kneezy!

Tap your head..., clap your hands..., touch your nose..., cross your legs... (which, if you do it when bending your knees, will mean you all fall over!)

Colours and directions
(and the long igh sound)

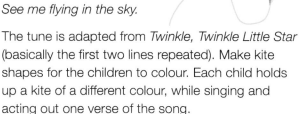

I'm a kite, a bright red kite
I fly to the left, I fly to the right
I start off low, I fly up high
See me flying in the sky.

The tune is adapted from *Twinkle, Twinkle Little Star* (basically the first two lines repeated). Make kite shapes for the children to colour. Each child holds up a kite of a different colour, while singing and acting out one verse of the song.

Quick and slow
(and the long oa sound)

Row, row, row the boat
Slow and slow can be
Row, row, row the boat
Slowly over the sea

Row, row, row the boat
Quick as quick can be
Row, row, row the boat
Quickly over the sea.

Sing to the original tune, making rowing actions. Vary the speed appropriately.

A counting rhyme
(and the long oo sound)

Oo oo dippity doo – how many tigers in the zoo?
I can count quite a few (count them, all together)
But there's only one kangaroo – 'boo hoo!'

Put children in groups of varying numbers and give each an animal identity, for example monkeys, penguins, pandas, parrots, lions. An adult can be the lonely kangaroo, saying 'Boo hoo' at the end of each verse.

Left-right brain interaction

Doing the *Hokey Cokey (You put your left arm in...)* and marching with the *Grand Old Duke of York* (left, right, left right) has taught many generations of children two important words – and the underlying concepts – needed to help develop L→R directionality in reading and writing.

However, there's more to left and right than that. Reading and writing are highly complex tasks, involving the integration of mental activity in both the left and right hemispheres of the brain. For instance, in order to read with understanding, a child must be able to combine:

- phonic decoding (the sort of small, sequential, analytic processing task associated with the left brain)

- overall comprehension of the text (the type of holistic understanding associated with the right brain).

Neural networks are extremely complex, depending on a vast range of neural interconnections within the brain – and body – as a whole, so in recent years simplistic left/right brain theories (such as those underpinning 'brain gym') have been given short shrift by neuroscientists.

Nevertheless, there is still plenty of scientific interest in the implications of our 'divided brain' (for a summary see McGilchrist, 2010), and much to be learned.

Music and language involve activity in specific parts of the brain, with music centred (mainly) in the right hemisphere and language (mainly) in the left. Throughout the ages, singing, dancing and moving to music have been important elements in human culture, and in the initiation of children into that culture. Physical activity that involves controlled and integrated movement of both sides of the body helps children develop connections between the two hemispheres. *The Hokey Cokey*, like other games and dances requiring cross-lateral movement, fulfils all these requirements, as does marching in time to a song. They also develop children's motor control and whole-body coordination in preparation for the physical skills of handwriting (see Chapter 7).

We do not think it a coincidence that Finland, which places great emphasis on music, song and dance during the early years, continually tops the literacy charts in the western world.

Activities

All sorts of dance

- Provide a music area with plenty of music with a strong beat. Teach the children how to operate the CD player and encourage them to dance, dance, dance!

- Show children how to do a simple circle dance. If they have trouble staying together, provide a large piece of covered elastic that they can hold on to. (If you don't want to make your own, you can get one from JABADAO – see page 136).

- If any parents, grandparents or others in the school community are dancers, for example zumba, folk, ceilidh, ballroom or line-dancing, ask them to bring in some music and teach the children some of the simplest moves.

Left right, left right!

March, march, march, as you move from one place to another. Have a marching band and lead children in procession around the outside area. Make ankle bands by sewing bells to some elastic and let the children wear them as they march. This way, they will hear and feel the regular beat as they move. Provide regimental marching tunes for them to march to, and other marching music – pretend they're soldiers or cheer-leaders, whichever they prefer!

Bim, bam, boom

Provide plenty of opportunities for drumming. If you don't have conventional drums use old paint tins, saucepans, waste paper bins, dustbins etc. Tie off the ends of washing up mops and use as beaters.

Funky dance gym

Choose some lively music and make up actions to accompany it, including some that involve cross-over movements such as tapping the right shoulder with the left hand and vice versa. Demonstrate the dance to the children, then break it into sections to teach them the actions. Make sure it's good and funky, and that there's plenty of repetition. Sue particularly enjoys doing this to the theme tune from Rocky, which is suitable for plenty of 'boxing' and 'keep fit' movements.

Passing games

- Sit the children in a circle and give out three or four beanbags. As you sing, pass the beanbags around the circle, encouraging the children to pass them on the 'beat.'

- Use cuddly toys, and as you sing pass the toys around the circle. Adapt a well-known song as a passing song, for example *Here we go passing the ted around, ted around, ted around* (instead of going round the mulberry bush).

- Pass a tambourine around the circle. As each child receives the tambourine they bang it a specified number of times.

Also important for encouraging cross-over movements:

- Ensure that children have ongoing, daily access to a well-equipped outside area where they can engage in cross lateral movement naturally as they play.

- Facilitate opportunities for crawling by providing plenty of low tunnels. If you don't have any, open up the ends of cardboard boxes and join them together with parcel tape. Provide boxes and tape for the children to construct their own tunnels!

- Provide plenty of opportunities for children to walk across low balance bars and construct bridges for them to cross.

A musical setting

Early years practitioners have always recognized the crucial importance of music to the overall development of the child, but now that research into brain development is confirming what we have always intuitively known, it's even more important to pay serious attention to the quality of our provision for music. As well as teacher-initiated musical activities, there should be plenty of opportunities for children to expand their interest, involvement and skills through their own child-initiated music and song.

Listening to and making music

- Provide a listening centre where children can go to listen to a range of music from a variety of different cultures.

- Encourage children to develop their critical response and express their opinions with regard to which pieces of music and which songs they most like, and why.

- Take advantage of opportunities for the children to hear adults and older children singing and playing instruments.

- Provide high quality music areas (both inside and out if possible), where children can go to explore sound and handle instruments that can be beaten, shaken, blown or strummed. When children are working with sound makers, offer sensitive support and encouragement, asking questions which will steer them into offering their ideas about how the instruments might be used.

- Ensure children are taught how to care for the resources.

- Collect objects and materials (for example recycled household objects and packaging) which the children can use to make musical instruments.

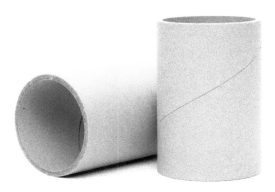

Songs and rhymes

- Try to ensure a balance between the teacher- and child-initiated singing, for example once you have taught the children a song, provide a CD player so that they can practise and refine it during periods of child-initiated learning.

- Invite children to choose which songs they would most like to sing, or rhymes to recite.

- Encourage children to have fun with language by making up their own songs, raps and jingles.

- When adults have modelled the possibilities, allow the children to take the lead and build on what they have seen and heard to make it their own.

Musical performance

- Provide a performance area where children can go to perform musical pieces, movement sequences and dances – this could easily be outside. Look for something to value in every effort.

- Provide a range of objects and fabrics, for example scarves, ribbon sticks, beanbags, lengths of material etc., so that children can develop movement ideas for moving to music.

- Encourage and help children to record their own songs and musical compositions.

- Occasionally video musical or dance performances, for children to watch themselves later.

Storytime!

In the past, to share in a story children had to listen. Whether gathered around a storyteller, drinking in the repetitive patterned language of the oral tradition, or listening to a storybook read aloud, children engaged with the story by ear. Today, however, almost half the nation's four-year-olds have a television in their bedrooms, and a growing number have handheld devices providing 'interactive' story-based entertainment.

Stories on screen are mostly visual – viewers watch the characters and the setting, following the plot with their eyes. For young television and DVD addicts, most stories have no spoken narrative thread – just fragmented dialogue, sound effects and background music. Indeed, they are often even unaware that the story has a beginning, middle and end – they experience it as a conceptual whole. And while many 'interactive' screen-based stories have a voiced narrative, young viewers are constantly distracted from the words because by touching the screen they can 'make things happen'.

There's no doubt that good illustrations (as in picture books) can support children in following a spoken narrative, but when images (especially rapidly moving images) become the predominant element of a 'story' they turn into a distraction rather than a support. Young children's engagement with screens is intellectually far less demanding than engagement with a story that is told or read to them.

This is perhaps why teachers have found that children reared on screen-based entertainment often have difficulty learning to read. We might teach them phonics and sight words, and demonstrate how to trawl through big books – but if the language of text is unfamiliar, the 'shape' of stories unknown, and their ears untrained to narrative, they find it hard to make sense of what we're doing. Later, when asked to write a story, they're at a loss, because stories on screen do not stimulate the imagination. Neither do they model the use of words to tell a tale, describe a setting or bring characters to life.

Indeed, there may be even more profound problems for children unversed in oral narrative at an early age. Some neuroscientists believe that the capacity for logical, rational thought is underpinned by our exposure to narrative during childhood. So, before formal literacy begins, it's more important than ever that we immerse children in 'story language' by replicating the activities of old: storytelling and reading aloud.

Storytelling: developing listening skills

Storytelling develops all aspects of listening. The adult storyteller, unhampered by a book, can make eye-contact with the children, modelling how to use facial and vocal expression, gesture and body language, to maintain their attention. The rhythmic, repetitive, patterned language of the oral tradition – along, hopefully, with plenty of audience participation – develop attention span and auditory memory. We therefore recommend that, at any time, you have a repertoire of at least four or five stories, to be told and retold, at least one each day.

To draw children under the spell of a story you can also use puppets, pictures and props. These, of course, also help the storyteller. For instance, if your story involves finding a number of items during a walk in the forest, you can have the items on your knee in a bag, ready to produce with a flourish. Or you can create a story map, with pictures of the main events, which acts as a prompt to you and an illustration for the audience. Each performance should also highlight the key elements of a story: beginning, middle and end; well-defined characters and settings.

Storytelling is a powerful way to develop children's speaking and listening skills, and anybody can do it! You don't have to be an extrovert, you don't need any special qualifications, and it doesn't matter if you make a mistake: the children will revel in your blunders and enjoy putting you right!

However, when you're first getting started it may help to rehearse. If you record your story – using plenty of key phrases and repetition – and listen to it several times (perhaps in the car driving to and from work, joining in as it becomes more familiar), you will soon commit it to memory.

Some traditional stories for telling:

- The Gingerbread Man
- Goldilocks and the Three Bears
- Red Riding Hood
- Three Billy Goats Gruff
- Jack and the Beanstalk
- The Little Red Hen
- Three Little Pigs
- The Enormous Turnip
- Rapunzel

These tales demonstrate the strengths of a good story – clear-cut characters (not too many and not too complex), repetition, build-up of the plot, good overcoming evil, a happy ending. However, the best stories are the ones you make up yourself, to fit the needs of the children you work with (see opposite).

Telling children stories

Soft toy stories

Soft toys make an excellent focus for storytelling because they engage children's emotions. Select a character that appeals to you, because this helps you believe in your character and tell your story well – if you don't believe in it, your listeners won't! Find a special bag from which to produce the toy when he makes his first appearance as this heightens the excitement. Tell the children that you have someone special that wants to meet them, then slowly reveal the toy. Floppy soft toys are best as they are easy to manipulate. Sit it on your hand and use your other hand to move the head as you tell your story about the character (practise in front of a mirror – you'll be amazed at the range of expressions you can achieve).

Puppet stories

All that has been said about soft toys also applies to puppets. Once you have one or two popular characters your stories can go on and on. You can create your own soap opera, and the more the children hear about your characters, the more they will want to hear!

Story sacks

These take time to put together, but if everyone contributes and the work is shared you can soon build up a collection (see Using Storysacks in the Resources section page 135). Or you can buy ready-made ones to go with picture books.

Make the most of your camera

Take your puppets and toys out into the community and the wider world and photograph them in different settings. Such photographs create the basis for many exciting stories. People will stare, but who cares!

Pictures and artefacts

You can also illustrate a story with picture cards, postcards or pictures from old calendars. A series of pictures can really spark the imagination. You can peg them along a washing line as the story progresses, to help children remember the sequence of events. Artefacts can be even more effective, as children can handle them as you tell the story. Start making a collection of interesting objects and let your imagination run wild!

Plots

Plots

When it comes to a plot, don't get complicated. Two important considerations are:

- A 'match of meaning' – in other words, whatever is happening to your character must match the children's experience in some way; they must be able to relate to it. That way, they will listen with real absorption.

- Making it memorable, so you (or a child) can tell it again – repetition is helpful here, for example going on a walk and finding/ doing various things, or meeting various people; a series of ways of solving a problem: First..., Next..., In the end...

When planning your story you may find this list of universal themes useful:

- Getting lost or losing something
- Getting into trouble
- Finding (an) interesting item(s)
- Feeling jealous
- Helping someone
- Being bullied/picked on
- Feeling afraid
- Winning and losing
- Split loyalties
- Mistaken identity
- Disappointment
- Accidents
- Making choices/moral conflict
- Not thinking ahead
- Disregarding/breaking rules

- Dishonesty
- Acting bravely; self-sacrifice
- Taking revenge
- Being surprised
- Getting locked in/trapped
- Endeavour
- Journeys and quests

Storytelling: developing speaking skills

Storytelling is a wonderful way of increasing children's vocabulary, sentence structure, and confidence. If you model storytelling, and also work with the children, crafting stories together (see opposite) they will soon become confident and adventurous storytellers themselves. Once individuals are ready to tell their own stories, a storyteller's chair or hat makes the experience really special. For many children this will be the first opportunity to speak uninterrupted for any length of time – a great confidence boost.

From the point of view of literacy-development, storytelling has a further advantage for children. It familiarises them with 'story grammar' – the key ingredients and 'shape' of a story. Listening to lots of stories and making up their own mean that, when they eventually come to write stories, they will not have to struggle to invent characters, settings and plots.

And storytelling does not have to mean fiction. We all have real-life stories to tell, and children can be encouraged to tell stories about themselves – holiday adventures, anecdotes about 'when they were little', or accounts of events connected to a topic under study. Storytelling can become a regular feature of partnered work: Tell your story to your partner... after which a few stories can be shared with the whole class.

Learning stories by heart

Listening to adults telling stories can lead to another type of spoken language: recitation. For children unfamiliar with stories, this can be deeply satisfying. It also develops auditory memory and familiarises children with key sentence constructions. This is why we recommend the repeated retelling of some favourite stories. After a few listening sessions, most children pick up and can be encouraged to join in with the story. If you encourage choral recitation, those with less well-developed auditory memory will be carried along by the rest. You can encourage recitation by devising simple actions to accompany key words and phrases, bringing in kinaesthetic memory, and drawing a simple story map.

Once a story is familiar, you can sit back, letting the children take over completely. If they lose the thread, you provide a prompt (the next phrase, an action, point to the story map...). Eventually you can encourage individuals to tell the story, either one-to-one or in a small group. Alternatively, children can tell a story to a talking partner, who takes on the role of the adult, prompting where necessary. By building a store of characters, plots and story-language in this way, children will find it easier to create their own stories, in role-play, storytelling sessions and, in later years, when they come to write.

> Watch out for children who do not join in, and provide more one-to-one interaction (see page 20) or perhaps opportunities to retell favourite stories in a group of two or three.

Children telling stories

The magic box

For this activity you need the cooperation of the parents. Explain to the children that they will take it in turns to take the magic box home and place it on the windowsill in their bedroom. When they wake up in the morning there will be something for them in the magic box. (Explain to parents that this need only be a small token.) The following morning the child brings the box back to school and tells everyone about what they found in the box.

The journey

You will need: some play people, animal figures, pictures from magazines depicting settings, vehicles and activities and a box of miscellaneous artefacts.

Sit the children in a circle with the resources in containers in the middle: characters, settings, vehicles, activities, objects. Explain that you are going to make up a story about some friends who go on a journey. Pass an object around the circle, explaining that whoever has the object when you give the signal gets to choose a character (the signal can be a bell, handclap, etc). Encourage the child who selects the character to set the scene, for example *Once upon a time there was a ...* Continue to pass around your object until the children have chosen and added to the spoken story another character, a place where they went, a vehicle for them to travel in and an activity that they took part in. Finally, on the way home they can find something (child chooses from the box of mixed artefacts). Model how the story might end, and once they have seen you do this a few times they will soon begin to do it for themselves.

The story bag

You will need: an attractive-looking bag and some interesting and unusual artefacts, for example an old key, magnifying glass, map, binoculars, a crystal or precious stone etc.

Tell the children that you are going to make up a story about the day Class X went on a very unusual school trip. Ask for suggestions for where the story may be set and how it might start. Invite children to take turns drawing an object out of the bag, and weaving a story about what happened when each item was found. If there are several suggestions have them consider which would be the most appropriate and if they become stuck offer a few suggestions of your own.

Our special character

One of the best ways to generate stories is to create your own character, arising from the children's interests. You could use a toy (a lonely teddy?) or even make a full-size model (some Scottish children made 'Mr Togs the Tailor' and he lived in a tailor's shop in their classroom for half a year!). The children can be involved in deciding: the character's name, where s/he lives (can you make it?) and who s/he lives with; the character's personality and what s/he likes doing. Once their characters have become established you can go on to create situations to which the children can respond, and in so doing, you may find the universal themes on the previous page helpful. Some useful starting points for children's stories are:

- taking your character in, covered in plasters or bandaged up – what happened?

- having your character upset because a favourite toy has been broken

- maybe your character is frightened because s/he has to go to the dentist

- having the character 'disappear' – where's s/he gone? (S/he could leave a note or send a postcard.)

Maybe the children could take it in turns to take the character home for the weekend and then tell the story of what took place during that time.

Reading aloud - five a day!

Lucky children learn to read 'naturally'. A parent or carer sits and shares favourite books time after time with the child joining in, until he or she can 'read along' (which is initially just reciting). Gradually, through years of this sort of pleasurable interaction, the child begins to recognise certain words and to associate letters with sounds. We can replicate this process by reading children at least five books every day, repeatedly returning to favourites, until pupils 'read along'. In a group, less able children are often supported in this by watching their peers, and we can help the learning process by sometimes setting the words to music or adding actions.

'Five a day' sessions should be at a regular time, and should not take long – perhaps ten to 15 minutes at the start of the day, after break or before home time. Short picture books with lots of repetition (for example *Where's Spot?, Farmer Duck, Handa's Surprise*) and rhyme and rhythm (for example *This is the Bear, We're Going On A Bear Hunt*) are ideal, and once children are familiar with them, should not take long to read. New books should be introduced into the 'five a day' routine gradually, perhaps one or two new ones per week.

One of these new books could be the 'Book of the week', which you read every day. When you introduce the 'Book of the week' you may want to spend some time talking about it, but thereafter don't interrupt the story with talk. Just read the book for fun and let it speak for itself! With frequent re-readings, children should be able to learn by heart at least ten storybooks a term, so eventually you can sit back, and let the group – or individual children – take the lead and 'read' the book.

'Five a day' develops many of the same skills as 'storytelling for literacy' (see pages 48-51) – especially auditory memory – but with an important bonus: children begin to internalise the patterns of written language. Familiarity with written sentence structures is, of course, essential before children can use grammatical cues to predict words in text, an important skill for reading. By Reception, in the early re-readings of stories, you can start to develop children's prediction skills orally by occasionally stopping as you read, and letting them fill in the missing word – but don't overdo this. The key element in reading aloud should always be pleasure: don't ever let it turn into a chore.

50 books for reading aloud

The most important factor in selecting a book to read aloud is that you enjoy reading it yourself. The following list is composed of tried and tested children's favourites.

Alfie Get In First Shirley Hughes (Red Fox)

Amazing Grace Mary Hoffman (Frances Lincoln)

Brown Bear, Brown Bear, What Do You See? Bill Martin Jnr and Eric Carle (Puffin)

Dear Daddy Philippe Dupasquier (Picture Puffin)

Dear Zoo Rod Campbell (Puffin)

Doctor Dog Babette Cole (Red Fox)

Dogger Shirley Hughes (Picture Lions)

Duck in the Truck Jez Alborough (Collins)

Each Peach Pear Plum Janet and Allan Ahlberg (Puffin)

Elmer David McKee (Red Fox)

Farmer Duck Martin Waddell (Walker)

Foggy Foggy Forest Nick Sharratt (Scholastic)

Funnybones Janet and Allan Ahlberg (Puffin)

Giraffes Can't Dance Giles Andreae (Orchard Books)

Gorilla Anthony Browne (Red Fox)

Hairy Maclary from Donaldson's Dairy Lynley Dodd (Puffin)

Handa's Surprise Eileen Browne (Walker)

Hector's New Trainers Amanda Vesey (Picture Lions)

Jamaica and Brianna Juanita Havill (Mammoth)

Little Rabbit Foo Foo Michael Rosen and Arthur Robbins (Walker)

My Cat Likes to Hide in Boxes Eve Sutton and Lynley Dodd (Puffin)

Mr Gumpy's Outing John Burningham (Red Fox)

Mr Magnolia Quentin Blake (Red Fox)

Not Now Bernard David McKee (Red Fox)

One Snowy Night Nick Butterworth (Collins)

Owl Babies Martin Waddell (Walker)

Pass It, Polly Sarah Garland (Puffin)

Pass the Jam, Jim Kaye Umansky and Margaret Chamberlain (Red Fox) *Peace at Last* Jill Murphy (MacMillan)

Peace at Last Jill Murphy (Macmillan)

Rosie's Walk Pat Hutchinson (Red Fox)

Some Dogs Do Jez Alborough (Walker Books)

Someone Bigger Jonathan Emmett (Oxford University Press)

So Much Trish Cooke (Walker Books)

Solo Paul Geraghty (Hutchinson)

Suddenly! Colin McNaughton (Collins)

Tall Inside Jean Richardson (Picture Puffins)

The Bear Under the Stairs Helen Cooper (Corgi)

The Elephant and the Bad Baby Elfrida Vipont and Raymond Briggs (Puffin)

The Gingerbread Boy Ian Beck (Oxford University Press)

The Gruffalo Julia Donaldson (MacMillan Children's Books)

The Tiger Who Came to Tea Judith Kerr (Collins)

The Train Ride June Crebbin and Stephen Lambert (Walker)

The Very Hungry Caterpillar Eric Carle (Puffin)

This is the Bear and the Bad Little Girl Sarah Hayes (Walker)

Through My Window Tony Bradman and Eileen Browne (Mammoth)

Tortoise's Dream Joanna Troughton (Puffin)

We're Going on a Bear Hunt Michael Rosen and Helen Oxenbury (Walker)

Where the Wild Things Are Maurice Sendak (Red Fox)

What's in the Witch's Kitchen? Nick Sharratt (Walker Books)

Where's My Teddy? Jez Alborough (Walker)

Developing imaginative engagement

Stories, told or read, provide the basis for many imaginative activities – all of which develop spoken language skills and children's ability to engage with stories and with each other.

- **Drama:** help the children to turn the story into a play, taking turns to play the parts of the characters (perhaps – if they know the story by heart – the rest of the group could act as choral narrators). In the early stages, this may need modelling (see page 36). Plays may be totally informal, or children can devise their own costumes, props and scenery and turn it into a full-scale performance.

- **Role-play:** this will happen naturally, but you can encourage it by providing the props and dressing-up clothes that will help transform the role-play area into the three bears' house, the giant's castle, and so on. Of course, role-play doesn't need to happen in the 'corner' – a few carefully-arranged chairs or boxes can become the 'Train Ride', any room can be transformed into the landscape of the 'Bear Hunt', and so on.

- **Retelling:** story maps, time lines, small world or fuzzy felt characters, masks, puppets, soft toys and so on all encourage children to retell stories. Pictures in old copies of a favourite book can be cut out and used as prompts for retelling. A collection of suitable artefacts, along with a copy of the book, can be made into a story sack, to be taken home and shared with parents.

- **Hot-seating:** older children love dressing up as favourite characters and sitting in the 'hot-seat' to answer questions from the rest of the group. It's also great fun if adults sometimes dress up and sit in the 'hot-seat', and tends to encourage lots of questioning.

- **Artwork:** well-loved stories can be transformed into pictures, friezes, small world settings, collages, storybooks. Working on these imaginative reconstructions provides many opportunities to return to key vocabulary and to talk about the who, what, where and why of the story.

- **Music, song, dance:** stories or parts of stories can also be turned into action songs, set to music, turned into mimes and dances – see Chapter 3.

Prop boxes for re-enacting stories

Make collections of dressing-up clothes and artefacts to enable children to further explore the ideas and vocabulary introduced during an adult-initiated storytime, for example

- **The Three Bears**: a golden wig for Goldilocks; masks for the bears; cones or posts for trees; three bowls and spoons; some porridge oats; three small chairs, three pieces of carpet for the beds. Make a laminated sign: The three bears cottage. Include the song *When Goldilocks went to the House of the Bears* and published versions of the story.

- **Jack and the Beanstalk**: a very long rope; some pebbles; a packet of seeds; some large boots and a golden egg. Make some laminated signs saying: The giant's castle, The beanstalk, Jack's house.

Make labels to denote characters in the story. Laminate them, punch holes in them and thread string through the holes. The children really enjoy wearing the label that matches the character they are playing. Prop boxes are excellent for use outside and stretch the children's imaginations more than a 'static' role-play corner set up inside. The outdoor environment also opens up all kinds of possibilities for acting out stories that would be too messy (or noisy!) inside.

Story treasure hunt

Collect objects that appear in a story you share with the children, for example if you focus on *Whatever Next?* by Jill Murphy it could be: some wellington boots, a colander, a teddy bear, an apple, a toy owl etc. Hide these objects in the outside area for the children to find.

Scaffolding children's dramatic play

Perhaps the most powerful thing practitioners can do is to role-play stories with the children. At first children may only take on a small part in the story, but as they watch the adults and gain in confidence they will take on more and more for themselves!

Masks and puppets

Build up a collection of masks – some stories lend themselves really well to being re-enacted with masks, for example *The Gingerbread Boy, The Three Billy Goats Gruff* and *Where The Wild Things Are* by Maurice Sendak. And all role-play can be carried out on a smaller scale with puppets. Children can make their own, but a suitable collection of hand puppets is ideal for acting out a story like *One Snowy Night* by Nick Butterworth.

Small world play

Set up a small world scenario that enables children to explore a story further, for example if you were focusing on *We're Going On A Bear Hunt* by Michael Rosen you might use a series of unused cat litter trays to represent each stage of the story. (These are extremely cheap to buy and can be used for a wide range of purposes!). In the first tray, sow grass seed in compost to make the long wavy grass. In the second, put pebbles and shallow water to represent the river. In the third, use clay or compost to represent the mud. In the fourth, stick twigs into lumps of Plasticine to represent the forest. In the fifth, use cotton wool and tin foil to represent the snowstorm. Finally, build a small cave for your bear. Heavy material with a dim lamp inside can be really effective! Use play people to represent the family and buy an extra copy of the book to cut up and laminate so the children can sequence the text to match the stages of the story.

Make your own picture

This is an important listening activity, since it encourages 'mental imaging', which will be important when children come to write stories themselves. Start with a very short vivid story or poem. Explain that you're not going to show them a picture as you read today – you want them to focus on a blank area (empty whiteboard? blank wall?) and 'make your own pictures in your heads'. When you've read the story/poem ask what pictures they conjured up. Don't be surprised if at first, few respond – children who are constantly fed images on television often do not know how to image in their heads. Talk about the 'pictures in their heads' and ask them to paint or draw their pictures. Repeat the activity, gradually choosing lengthier texts.

Nurturing children's imaginations

Storytelling and listening to stories are key ways of stimulating children's imaginative powers and, as we have illustrated, stories provide a rich context for drama, role-play and other creative activities. However, there are many other ways of nurturing children's imagination and stimulating their language, which may also lead into story-making or the writing of a group poem.

◼ What's in the bag?

You need: a feely bag with something interesting inside, for example some dough inside a plastic bag; some flour secured in a plastic bag; or some sugar cubes or marbles. The children sit in a circle and the bag is passed around for them to feel. If it reminds them of anything, if they think they know what it is or if they have a thought to share (or a word to describe what they feel), they speak before they pass the bag on.

◼ Play in the field of light

You need: a dark den created from a tent or cardboard boxes, drapes and blankets; objects to move into the field of light (for instance, coloured slides, natural materials and items suggested by the children) and torches to create the field of light. Talk with the children about all the things it makes them think about and if appropriate, build on their ideas.

◼ Branches and leaves

You need: branches and leaves that have been discarded when pruning hedges and trees and some suitable music. Play the music and let the children move the branches through space to explore what they will do (having talked through the safety issues with them first!). Generate ideas for other ways in which the branches could be used for example to make a den or a shelter, or to role-play a wood or an enchanted forest. Imagine, create and build a story.

◼ Cardboard boxes

You need: a selection of cardboard boxes with holes cut in the sides and top so that the children can 'wear' them. The children take turns to 'dress up' in the boxes and use them in any way they like. Share ideas about some of the things they could be used for. The children observing can see if they can guess what is being represented.

◼ Duvet movements

You need: an old duvet cover and a P.E. mat if one is available. Spread the duvet cover out on top of the P.E. mat and get the children to sit around the sides. A few at a time, they can get inside the duvet cover and explore different movements. Encourage the children who are watching to share their ideas about what they were thinking about as they observe the 'movers'.

◼ Fast and slow music

You need: rolls of paper, for example old wallpaper, markers and a pre-recorded CD of contrasting music i.e. slow and gentle, up beat and loud, choral, classical, jazz, latin etc. Play the music and encourage the children to experience it in any way they like. Some may want to dance and move around the room, whereas others may prefer to use the markers and draw their response. Incorporate the use of fabrics if desired and talk with the children about their thoughts and experiences.

Learning about print

As long as children have plenty of experience of interactive language, learning to talk is an entirely natural process. In the preceding chapters, we've described many activities designed to build on natural language development – increasing children's spoken vocabulary and ability to express their ideas in words.

However, literacy is not natural – reading involves the patterning of complex intellectual behaviour, employing a range of visual, auditory and cognitive skills. Some lucky children learn to read apparently effortlessly through sharing plenty of books with adults – and our 'five a day' routine is designed to exploit this pleasurable way of learning – but we cannot assume this will happen. Many children need a great deal of structured teaching. As for learning to write, which is even more complex – and requires in addition quite taxing physical coordination of hand and eye movements – this is hardly ever 'picked up': all children need careful teaching. The remaining chapters of this book cover aspects of written language with which children must be familiar before they can learn to read and write – and the first of these is awareness of the print itself.

To many young children print is invisible – it is so meaningless to them that they don't even notice it. To others it is merely one sort of mysterious squiggle among many – including the patterns on the wallpaper. Children have to learn that print is significant. They have to recognise that writing is different from pictures, that words and letters are different from numbers. As soon as they start noticing print, those italicised words are important vocabulary to use in context whenever possible.

They also have to know what reading and writing is for, and how people do it – for instance, that in English print goes from left to right and from the top to the bottom of the page. Finally, they must be familiar with the letters of the alphabet, and how these are used to represent words (see Chapter 6). Helping children recognise the nature and functions of print is an important element in laying the foundations of literacy.

Awareness of print

The best introduction to 'the nature and functions of print' is to draw attention to the many examples of environmental print which have significance for children in their daily lives. These can be found both inside school and out, and are powerful real-life illustrations of the importance of print. The 'listening walks' suggested in the first chapter could double as 'print walks', and children's attention be drawn to common notices relevant to them, for example *Stop, Exit, Fire Exit, Toilets, Playground, Shop, Open, Menu*. Adults should read the words aloud, talk about the sign and why it's there and ensure children know exactly what it means.

The same examples of environmental print (for example *Fire Exit*), preferably printed exactly like the conventional sign, should also be displayed wherever relevant in the classroom, at child height. They should also be integrated as often as possible into role-play areas (see opposite for examples). Some signs and notices occur in many contexts, and once children become aware of them, they often take great pleasure in spotting and 'reading' familiar signs for themselves. For many, these become the first 'sight words' – note how the word out appears in several common contexts (as a direction, and in the signs for *Checkout, Keep out, Out of order*). A child who is familiar with the word in one context can be helped to spot it in lots of others.

Once children have begun to develop phonological awareness, you can also point out initial letter sounds on print walks and in role-play, for example P for parking, L for learner, I for information, S and P on salt and pepper pots, B & B for Bed and Breakfast, H and C on taps, M for McDonalds, and so on.

Key environmental print

Shop

OPEN

NO DOGS

Shop

Sale

CLOSED

Trolley return

Any public building
(including school!)

EXIT

DO NOT BLOCK
FIRE EXIT

Lift

PUSH

PULL

TOILET

Outdoor signs

School ❯

STOP

NO PARKING

NO ENTRY

Bus Stop

FOR SALE

Restaurant/café, etc

Café

menu

FISH & CHIPS

SNACKS

Ice Cream

RESTAURANT

Alphabet knowledge

An important part of awareness of print is recognising and being able to name the letters of the alphabet, so it helps to teach children to recite the alphabet as soon as they're able to do so. The easiest way to do this is through an alphabet song. Once they can sing along, link it to an alphabet chart, displayed at child height in the setting. Sing the song, pointing to the letters on the chart, and encouraging children to join in. After a while, hand over the pointing to volunteers.

Refer to the letters by their alphabet names (ay, bee, cee) – at this stage, alphabet knowledge has nothing to do with phonics, so this is not a case of /k/ for cat. Familiarisation with the alphabet ensures that children know what letters are, and also that there are a limited number of them (two versions of each letter: capital and lower case). Without this knowledge, learning to read could seem an impossibly daunting task.

If children are interested – especially in the letters of their own names – they'll want to play with the shapes, decorating letters, making prints or playdough lettershapes and so on. Most children are also keen to write their name and, if so, should be helped to do so, but that's as far as writing letters should go in the early stages. Long-term success in writing requires adequate fine motor control, hand-eye coordination and control of the muscles of the fingers, and starting too early can do more harm than good – see Chapter 7.

The more children play with the letters before learning about reading and writing begins in earnest, the more confident and competent they'll be when they start phonics and, eventually, handwriting.

Dough alphabet

You need: loads of dough, some alphabet cutters and a laminated alphabet strip.

As you observe the children playing with the cutters you will be able to learn much about their awareness of print. Encourage those who are ready to match the letters they are making to the alphabet strip. Some of the children may want to make their names. Keep a range of alphabet books nearby so that the children can link their experiences, and sing the alphabet song as you work to encourage yet more links.

Alphabet washing line

You need: an alphabet frieze, some card, a line and some pegs.

Cut up the alphabet frieze, stick the letters onto card and laminate them. (You could have upper case letters on one side and lower case letters on the other.) This way, children can use the frieze to make their names, sequence letters and make up simple slogans. The added bonus of having well laminated cards is that they can be used outside.

Make your own alphabet book

The children are the 'stars' of this book, so they will be motivated to look at it closely. Get the children to make collections of things that begin with A, B and C etc. The children who have names beginning with A then have their photograph taken with the collection they have made, and so on through the alphabet. If you have a class mascot or puppet, include him/her in the photographs as this adds even more engagement to the process. This book can then be placed in the book corner and the children encouraged to take it home. In fact, try stopping them, when it features them and all their friends!

Alphabet treasure hunt

You need: wooden or plastic letters and plenty of sand or compost in which to bury the letters.

The children could be set the challenge of finding the letters of their name. If they are not developmentally ready to do this they will just enjoy hunting for the letters and will increase their awareness of the alphabet.

The alphabet thief

You need: wooden, plastic or magnetic letters.

Lay the letters out in sequence with gaps where the missing letters should be. Tell the children that someone or something has removed the letters and that an urgent search is required. Prior to doing this you will of course have hidden the missing letters around the setting. This is a great activity for outdoors as the letters can be tied to the branches of trees and hidden under stones etc. Hold a celebration when all the letters have been recovered and placed in the correct order.

Sweetshop alphabet

For this activity you will need to get the children to collect as many sweet and chocolate wrappers as they can. You will also need a scrapbook. Talk with the children about which sweets begin with which letter and begin to compile the scrapbook. Don't worry too much if you can't find a wrapper for every letter.

Concepts about literacy

In Chapter 4 we suggested repeated reading ('five a day') of storybooks aloud. With frequent exposure to books in this way, opportunities to look at books themselves in the book corner, and to make their own picture books based on familiar stories and their own experiences, most children will learn all they need to know about 'how books work'. If a few 'five a day' books are available in 'big book' versions, you can sometimes demonstrate some aspects more overtly – for instance, running a finger under the text to illustrate the left-right directionality of print.

However, as well as fiction, children also need you to share and model reading a range of other texts in meaningful contexts – recipes, posters, letters, lunch menus, information books and so on – demonstrating what they're for and how they're organised. Try to take advantage of every opportunity to demonstrate how and why adults read.

Demonstration is also the best way to teach underlying concepts about writing, and 'Shared writing' (described on page 89) should happen regularly, with children watching as you write labels and notices for the classroom, parts of letters to parents, captions for

pictures, and so on, giving a running commentary on what you are doing. In today's electronic world, many children seldom see adults writing by hand, so it's essential to provide many experiences while they're in the setting.

As they become aware of the significance of print, most children will incorporate reading and writing into their role-play – 'pretend reading' menus, leaflets and so on, and 'scribble-writing' notes and messages of various kinds. We can encourage and develop this by ensuring that role-play areas are suitably equipped with the relevant materials for literacy – health leaflets, posters, magazines, patient notes and 'prescription pads' in the doctor's surgery; brochures, maps, posters and timetables in the travel agents, etc.

While verisimilitude often requires relevant ICT equipment in role-play areas, in the early stages we believe it's not particularly helpful to encourage screen-based literacy skills. Children need plenty of real-life, three-dimensional, active experiences to develop the physical capacities that underpin reading and writing. A reliance too early on screens distracts them from these experiences.

Activities

The message board

Use a whiteboard or similar, specially designated for notes about issues important to the children. When children arrive anxious to tell you they have to go to the dentist, have party invitations to give out or something special to show, write a message on the message board to help you remember. Read it back to them, and when they nag about what they've asked you to do, refer them to the board.

Message boxes and pigeon holes

Buy a supply of 'shoe tidies' and stitch them into one large block that can be suspended from a curtain rail or broom handle. Make sure there are enough spaces for each child and adult to have their own. Stick laminated photographs of the children onto their space so they can identify their own pigeon hole. They can now use the pigeon holes to exchange tokens, notes and messages.

The abandoned toy

You need: a soft toy wrapped in a parcel and labelled Please help me!, and a letter explaining why the toy needs help.

Place the parcel somewhere in the outside area for the children to discover. They are usually very excited when they find it. Read the letter inside and let the children dictate a reply. You can then respond to their reply and the correspondence can continue as long as the children remain interested, which is usually quite a long time.

The treasure hunt

You need: a 'treasure box' containing a small token and a message (for example a positive comment) for each child. Find a suitable place to hide it (if you're really adventurous and have a waterproof box, bury it in the outside area!).

Write a letter to the children explaining that there is hidden treasure and a message for them all – it could be from someone they know or a favourite storybook character. It should say that to find the treasure they will have to follow a series of clues, and give the location of the first clue. Write and hide the clues. Following the clues until the treasure is found could happen over a day or even a week. Make a display of the clues and the children's individual messages. They usually enjoy reading these to each other.

Activities

Television critics

Children are very interested in what has been and is going to be on television. Talk with the children about what's on television that night, and explain that once they've watched it, you're going to ask them what they thought about the programme. Note their responses on a large sheet of paper, which the children can later decorate with pictures cut from the television guide. In order to fully facilitate this activity you may need to view the programme yourself ... but it is all in a good cause.

Our special character
(continued from page 52)

Special characters (soft toys or homemade models) can become the focus of print-based activities. They may receive letters – such as invitations, postcards from friends, official letters requesting them to do something – which spark off another chapter in their adventure. As part of a story, they may need to write letters, lists, signs or notices; you can do this on their behalf. Alternatively, they may need to look up information — for instance in an atlas, reference book, telephone book or recipe book; you can read on their behalf too. It may be necessary to provide them with documentation – a passport and tickets for a foreign holiday; birth and wedding certificates for happy events; a police statement form in the event of a crime. If they go on holiday, they will probably want to send postcards; on longer trips they may be regular letter-writers.

Cut-out messages

You need a large collection of boxes and wrappers from favourite food.

Explain to the children that they are going to cut out words and letters from the wrappers to use as part of a list, poster or notice. Talk about the ways in which the packaging could be used and explore all the various forms of print and text. This is a valuable process in itself and usually generates lots of talk, with the children often noticing subtleties of the packaging of which adults aren't aware. Once you have decided how to use the wrappers, begin cutting and formulate your message.

Sight words

One of the great problems in teaching literacy skills in English is that, due to the vagaries of our spelling system, many commonly-used words cannot be decoded or encoded phonetically. Overall, research suggests that the best introduction to reading and writing is through phonics. How, then, does one deal with the fact that words like 'the', 'said' and 'come' are phonetically irregular? These words must be recognised as wholes, and are commonly called 'sight words'.

It can be confusing if we draw attention to sight words and phonics at the same time. In terms of explaining how to read and write it is probably best to stick in the early stages to the phonic route, which we outline in the next chapter. However, once children have some grasp of phonics and want to read and write for themselves, no matter how carefully we select material, they will soon come up against words that have to be dealt with as whole words.

Children who are frequently read to, and who are used to responding to environmental print, often absorb these commonly-used words effortlessly. However, final preparation for formal reading should include:

- explaining to children that for some common words phonics doesn't work, and they have to remember how to recognise and spell them as wholes

- games and activities to ensure that all children are familiar with the main sight words (especially those that appear in books they will be reading).

Activities

To absorb words into the visual memory children need to see them in a variety of contexts, and some children need many more exposures to those words than others. Games are an engaging and fun way of ensuring that exposure and repetition.

Word hunt

You need a set of words for each child and a duplicate set that have been hidden in a variety of places.

Children can work individually or collaboratively, and the words can be tailored to their individual or collective needs. Once equipped with their words they set off to find the duplicates. This is a great game for outdoors!

Card games

These are real old favourites, but the children really do enjoy playing them. Make sight words into bingo, snap and happy families games.

Eat your words!

You need: some gingerbread dough and some bits and pieces for decorating biscuits.

Give each child in the group a word that you want them to add to their sight vocabulary. Let them make their words from the dough and decorate them. Once they have been cooked they can be displayed and read before they are eaten.

Once eaten, the children can recall who ate which word and find those words in the word bank or on the word wall.

The secret message

You need: a secret message written in black, which includes some important sight words written in red. (The black words are exposed but the sight words are covered.) The message could give instructions for how to find something that's been lost, to locate hidden treasure or to find out some important information.

Explain to the children that in order to 'crack the message' they must carry out certain tasks, and each time they complete a task they can uncover one of the words. (You can support the development of a sight vocabulary even further by giving tasks associated with specific words, for example *find the word 'they' in five places in the classroom...find the word 'said' in five different books.... find the five 'you' cards that are hidden in the classroom*). When all the tasks have been carried out and the hidden words uncovered the children can finally read the message. This activity works well when everyone gets some sort of treat at the end of it. For example, the message might read: *Go and look behind the cupboard and you will find something that you will like very much!'* or, '*On Friday you can all bring something from home that you would like to show to show to the rest of the class*'.

Joined-up memory

Sight words must also be learned as wholes for writing. By the time they are introduced, which we believe should be towards the end of the *Foundations of Literacy* programme, most children should be accustomed to writing simple phonically-regular words on individual whiteboards. Practising writing sight words as wholes – i.e., not sounding them out – exploits the kinesthetic learning channel, especially if children are able to write them as joined units. Plenty of practice writing the individual letter shapes (and perhaps joining common digraphs), should have prepared children to try a few joined words – see the teaching sequence below as an example. The teaching of joins should follow the usual pattern of movement from the shoulder, skywriting and finally practice on a whiteboard, all stages in which should be demonstrated, as described in Chapter 7. 'Grown up' joined-up writing is usually highly motivating for children.

$$he \rightarrow the \rightarrow they$$

Supporting children's involvement with print

The support provided by the early years practitioner can make the difference between children who simply develop an awareness of print and children who become so fascinated by it that they search for meaning with absorbed intent. Key features of quality support include the following.

■ Observe the children closely. Watch carefully and notice how children interact with text in all its forms. Notice what they are aware of and what they don't yet understand. Unless we do this, we cannot know what experiences to give them to help them expand their awareness of print.

■ Share your own experience with the children. Take in the books and magazines that are important to you. Talk with the children about how they give you pleasure and help you in your daily life.

■ Have books and print in all areas of the setting. Make sure you have text in the construction area, sand area and water area etc., and refer to these texts at every available opportunity. This sends out valuable messages about the importance of print.

■ Enable children to see their own words written down. Scribe on children's drawings and paintings (with their permission), and let them dictate messages and captions for displays, photographs and home-made books.

■ Encourage children to notice print and use writing in their play. When you set up any play scenario, mirror the text that would exist in the real world, for example home corners should always include calendars, magazines and comics, telephone directories, television magazines etc.

■ Include print in the outside area. Laminate posters, for example of trees, plants and insects to be found in the environment, and screw blackboards to the wall for writing messages.

■ Write down what children plan to do during periods of child-initiated learning. Talk to children about what they plan and write it on a self-adhesive label so they can wear it. It's a really powerful experience when other adults read the label and say, So you're going to play in the sand today! At first they ask, 'How do you know that?' They soon work it out!

■ Encourage book-making activities. Involve the children in making your own books (like the alphabet book described on page 63). You can make books of children's pictures with your scribed captions, scrapbooks of topics you study, and records of outings and activities illustrated with photographs taken with the digital camera. Where appropriate, give your book page numbers, a front cover, a contents pages and back cover 'blurb' (about the content and authors!)

■ Let children see you writing as often as possible. Children learn best from the people they love and respect, and because their key adults are very important to them, they will want to know, understand and copy the things that they do.

■ Talk about what you write with the children. Whether you are writing a message to another member of staff, filling in a report or recording an observation, tell the children what you are doing and why you are doing it. This will help them to understand that print is something important that helps us to organise our lives. Show them your shopping list and your 'Things to do' list. Get other adults to talk with the children about the things they read and write.

Chapter 6

Tuning into sound

About 25 years ago, there was a huge change in the way we treat small children. Until then, if a baby or toddler was crotchety, its parent had to pick him/her up, and talk or sing to calm him/her down. What sort of language did parents choose on these occasions? Nursery rhymes and songs, of course – repetitive patterned language which just happens to be ideal for tuning a young child's ears to the sounds of speech.

Nowadays, there's another option. After the briefest of cuddles, you might prop the child up in front of the television and put on a cartoon. Children love the bright colours and moving images – but the soundtrack is generally lost on them. Nowadays we tune our children into images, not sounds.

It's just as well our education system brought back the teaching of phonics – without this explicit attention to the sounds that make up words, very many children in the last five years may never have learned to read and write at all. However, we still have some way to go in successfully preparing children for phonics teaching. There are a number of developmental stages preceding 'phonemic awareness' (the point at which children implicitly understand that you can take a word apart and put it together again: /d/ /o/ /g/ = dog), which children from 'language-poor' backgrounds may not have experienced.

Trying to rush children through these developmental stages – or just 'leapfrogging' over them – is likely to cause problems in the long run. Hence our insistence on a rich diet of play, talk, story and song before phonics teaching begins – and continuing once it has begun. We also believe firmly that:

- practitioners should use their professional judgement as to when children are ready to benefit from phonics lessons

- early phonics-teaching should be fun, fast and multi-sensory, and conducted in small groups, as opposed to a whole-class activity.

A child who is clearly bewildered or distressed by an activity is unlikely to learn very much, and recent international research suggests that there really is no need to rush into formal teaching of literacy skills (see Introduction). At present, far too many children are being deprived of essential developmental experiences – a sedentary, screen-based home life is accompanied by ever earlier pressure for 'school readiness', which leaves little time or opportunity for the true foundations of literacy to be laid. They need plenty of the experiences described in Chapters 1 to 4 to tune into language – and to become aware of the individual speech sounds that make up language – before explicit teaching about the sound-symbol system of written English begins.

Phonological awareness

Phonological awareness means awareness of sounds in language, and is an essential precursor of phonemic awareness – the ability to discriminate individual speech sounds. Children go through a number of developmental stages in phonological awareness:

* awareness of words as units of sound. For children from 'language rich' homes, this happens naturally within the first couple of years, through constant exposure to interactive language. For others, the activities described in Chapters 1 to 4 should ensure they rapidly reach this stage.

* awareness of syllables, i.e. the recognition that words can consist of more than one sound. Again, for children who engage in plenty of talk, language play and song with adults, this should happen naturally, but the work on 'steady beat' described on pages 38-40 is particularly helpful.

* awareness of rhyme (see opposite).

These 'awarenesses' are completely implicit – children are not aware that they are aware! We can tell that they have reached a certain stage by their linguistic behaviour, especially the degree of pleasure they take in language play.

Rhyme and rhythm

By the time children are able to speak and listen at a level appropriate for the average three-year-old (see Appendix 1) they are usually aware of rhyme. They enjoy joining in with and learning to recite simple rhymes, and also delight in making up their own (*'It's easy, weasy, peasy, deasy!'*, *'This is Mr Ooly, Pooly, Dooly, Wooly'*). This is the beginning of phonemic awareness, because the child is gradually alerted to initial sounds (in the examples above, w, p, d and p, d, w). We should therefore provide, throughout the EYFS, daily opportunities to join in with, learn and recite rhymes. Appreciation and enjoyment of rhythm underpins awareness of rhyme, and accompanying actions can help make rhymes memorable, so the activities described in Chapter 3 are also very important.

Children who (despite a language-rich environment and language development appropriate to a three-year-old) do not begin to enjoy and play with rhyme, may have a specific learning difficulty (dyslexia). We can now detect such problems early, so refer any child who worries you to an educational psychologist.

Activities

Down on the farm

You need: A set of picture cards of different animals.

Shuffle the cards and give one to each child. Explain to the children that once they have looked at their picture they are to put it face down on their chair or on the floor. On a signal from you they are to stand up and make the noise of their animal. Explain that the object of the exercise is to find the people who are the same animal as they are. Talk about what they will need to do in order to do this effectively. You can play this game using zoo animals, vehicles, instruments etc. When children start learning phonics, you can adapt it to use with phonemes.

Stories in rhyme

One enjoyable way of developing children's phonological awareness is to include stories written in rhyme in your 'five a day' books. After a few readings they will be joining in, and when they know the text well you can stop reading at certain key points, allowing them to fill the gaps from memory. You will probably have many such texts in your setting, but some particularly useful ones are:

Bearobics Emily Bolam and Vic Parker (Hodder Children's Books)

Commotion In The Ocean Giles Andreae and David Wojtowycz (Orchard)

Five Little Ducks Ian Beck (Orchard)

Five Little Men in a Flying Saucer illustrated by Dan Crisp (Child's Play)

Octopus Socktopus Nick Sharratt (Alison Green Books, Scholastic)

Over In The Meadow Louise Voce (Walker Books)

Pants Nick Sharratt (Orchard)

Row Your Boat Pippa Goodhart (Picture Mammoth)

The Animal Boogie Debbie Harter (Barefoot Paperback)

The Fish Who Could Wish John Bush and Korky Paul (Oxford University Press)

The Lion Who Wanted to Love Giles Andreae and David Wojtowycz (Orchard Books)

Rhymes throughout the day

Make up simple rhymes that can be used
throughout the day, for example

At welcome time:

Hello *(insert child's name)*, how are you today?
It's really nice to see you, is what I'd like to say!

At transition times:

And now it's time to learn some more
So reach up to the sky, then touch the floor.
Wiggle your fingers and tap your knees
Then clap your hands with a ONE, TWO, THREE!

Prior to child-initiated learning:

Who is going to the sand today?
Who is going to the sand?
Who is going to the sand today?
Raise your hand and say!
I am going to the sand today,
I am going to the sand.
I am going to the sand today,
I'm going to the sand to play.

At tidy up time:

Now we have reached that time
When all the things are put away.
So mind that you all do your share
Because if you don't it won't be fair!

Find a rhyme and make me squeak

You need: a toy or puppet with a soundmaker
inside (pet shops are a particularly good source).

Sit the children in a circle and encourage them to
be inventive and make up words. It doesn't matter
if the word is a nonsense word, the skill is to hear
the pattern and repeat it. Choose a pattern that has
plenty of rhymes, for example cat, hat, mat, pat, rat,
or grumpy, lumpy, bumpy, jumpy etc and each time
someone thinks of a rhyme the puppet or toy can
'squeak' its appreciation.

Phonemic awareness

You can never do enough rhyming activities! However, once children are aware of rhyme, phonemic awareness will also be developed through alliterative games, tongue twisters and any activities requiring the clear articulation of individual speech sounds. While this can sometimes be done with a large group, discriminative listening really requires small group attention. All children therefore need regular small group work with an adult – and those whose progress is particularly slow need one-to-one attention.

The general activities outlined previously are only a starting point. Gradually we have to ensure children can hear and articulate (and eventually remember) the 44 phonemes used in the English language – see Appendix 3. The 'Jolly Phonics' technique of associating each sound with an action is a good way to tackle this, as long as it is kept playful and doesn't just turn in to 'phonic drill'.

For most children, the Reception year is quite early enough to start. If children are developmentally ready to hear the sounds, they should be able to pick up three or four phonemes and their related actions the first day. You can then return to these daily, playing 'I'll make a sound, you make the action' and adding further sounds as often as seems appropriate. Once sounds are familiar, you can also play 'I'll make the action, you make the sound'. It's important to keep careful records of the sounds you have covered, and of individual children's progress. Note that at this stage, we are talking about exclusively oral activities, not matching sounds to letters.

Right from the beginning, we also need to emphasize segmentation and blending – using the phonemes to 'sound out' words orally, for children to guess what the word is. These could be simple words like /k/ /a/ /t/ (cat) or children's names like /k/ /l/ /oa/ /i/ (Chloe). As long as these activities are entirely oral, it doesn't matter how words are spelled. Children should also be encouraged to sound out simple words or names in the same way. They also need games to help them discriminate individual sounds in a word, for example hearing the final sound.

Activities

What's in the bag?

You need: a feely bag with some objects inside. (The objects you choose will depend on the phonemes on which you wish to focus.)

Sit the children in a circle and pass the bag around the circle. When you shout 'stop' or give a similar signal, the child holding the bag draws out an object. They then name the object and pass it onto the next child who tries to think of something else beginning with the same sound. (If they cannot think of anything they pass the object to the next child.) The object continues around the circle until all the options have been exhausted.

The phoneme walk

You need: a puppet or soft toy and a camera. Explain to the children that they need to help the puppet to learn some phonemes.

Decide which phonemes you wish to focus on, then set off on your walk. Encourage the children to find things to show the puppet that begin with that particular phoneme. Use the camera to record the objects they find for future reference.

Wake up the puppet

Explain to the children that your puppet has fallen asleep and can only be woken up when they label an object by its beginning (or final) sound. Show them the object in question and get them to whisper the sound, gradually becoming louder and louder until the puppet wakes up.

The toybox

Make a collection of things from around your setting and put them all into a box.

Sit the children in a circle and explain that the object of the exercise is to sort out the things in the box according to their initial sound. Pass an object around the circle and on a signal from you they stop passing. The child with the object selects an item from the box and the game continues until all the items have been sorted.

Segment and move

For this activity, explain to the children that you are going to give them a movement instruction and that you are going to say it bit by bit. Further explain that they are to blend the sounds together to find out what you want them to do, for example, h/o/p, r/u/n, s/k/i/p etc. Alternatively, sit the children in a circle and put a collection of objects in the middle. As you segment the sounds the children take it in turns to identify the object you are referring to.

Change seats

You need: picture cards beginning with a variety of phonemes.

Sit the children in a circle and shout out instructions, for example everyone who has a picture of something beginning with... change seats. Get the children to continue changing seats until all those children who have pictures of things beginning with the same phoneme are sitting together. You can adapt this game according to the level of phonemic awareness you wish to address, for example:

- all those children who have a word with /a/ in the middle change seats

- all those children who have a word that ends with /n/ change seats.

There are many oral phonemic awareness games available from the Primary National Strategy: Playing with Sound and Progression in Phonics (DfES publications line: 0845 6022260).

Phonics: sound-symbol associations

The phonemes of English and the main ways in which they are represented, are given in Appendix 3. Once children can discriminate, articulate and remember a range of speech sounds (say, the sounds /k/ /a/ /t/ /p/ /i/ /n/ /s/) they should be ready to learn – through games and fun activities – to associate these sounds with specific letters or groups of letters. But always ensure that a phoneme is well-established orally before introducing the symbol, and if children do not seem to enjoy the phonic games, go back to oral work till you feel they are secure.

Symbols can be introduced using magnetic letters, lettercards, phonix cubes and so on. Again, segmenting and blending are an essential element – magnetic letters and phonix cubes are great for this. The main consideration, however, is that the process should be fun. Bored or bewildered children learn only one thing – how to switch off.

Once a sound-symbol relationship is well established, move away from 'Jolly Phonics' action, and integrate kinaesthetic learning through large-scale drawing of the letter-shapes, such as skywriting (see page 69). Eventually, when children have acquired good hand-eye coordination and pencil grip, sounds and words can be written (large) on individual whiteboards (see page 69).

All phonics teaching requires careful planning and record-keeping. The children needn't know how structured teaching is, but the practitioner should be working with almost military precision! Obviously there isn't room in this short section to deal with the systematic and thorough teaching of phonic knowledge, but there are now many good commercial schemes on the market. Whatever scheme you choose, augment it with fun activities that engage the children's interest. Don't forget the balancing act between the needs of the child and the requirements of the curriculum:

- **on the one hand, phonics teaching must be fun, fast, multi-sensory and cumulative**

- **on the other, it has to be addressed daily and systematically!**

About 15 minutes a day is enough to ensure coverage, but – as the key to this sort of skills learning is 'little and often' – you can also use phonic songs and segmenting games to fill in odd moments, such as transition times, in a queue for dinner and so on.

Activities

Place your phoneme
(initial and final phonemes)

You need: a collection of objects and a bag of phoneme cards.

Get the children to sit in a circle and place the objects in the middle. Pass the bag around and when you shout 'stop!' the child holding the bag draws out a card. If they can place it next to an object that begins or ends with that phoneme, they do so. (If the child has difficulty the rest of the group can help out.) Otherwise, the card is discarded and you carry on passing the bag around.

Mystery presents
(segmenting and blending)

You need: items (phonically regular words, for example mug, brick, sheep) that have been wrapped and labelled with their initial phoneme.

Tell the children that you have been given some presents and that you want them to help you guess what they might be from the phoneme on each one. Sit the children in a circle and pass the presents round so that they can make their guesses. Record their guesses on the whiteboard, (they can help you to sound out the words) then open the presents to see how many they managed to guess correctly.

In the bag (oral segmentation)

You will need: a small bag for each child in the group.

Ask children to choose two objects from around the room, put them in their bag (without showing anyone else) and return to the group. Children take turns to take an object out of their bag, and hold it up for the others to see. With the group, say the name of the object, then help them work out how to break the name into phonemes, for example:

- pencil: /p/ /e/ /n/ /s/ /i/ /l/

- scissors: /s/ /i/ /s/ /o/ /s/

- truck: /t/ /r/ /u/ /k/

Don't worry about the spelling – this is an oral activity, which helps children familiarize themselves with the idea of segmenting and blending. Once they've broken the word down into individual sounds, always pronounce the whole word again.

Phonics in action

Sounds into writing

Alongside games and activities, illustrate how phonic knowledge is put to use during shared writing (for example: *I want to write 'dog'. Let's see if we can sound that word out: d-o-g. I know the letters for that*: writing: d...o...g) or when reading a regularly spelled word, for instance when pointing out environmental print (*You know what this says, don't you? – stop. See, it's /s/ /t/ /o/ /p/.*) Do take care, though, not to let phonic encoding take over in any context to the extent that it swamps the meaning.

Gosh! That's what it's for!

Once children have acquired a reasonable level of phonic knowledge, they usually enjoy decoding some phonetically regular material – it can be quite a thrill suddenly to realize what all these sounds and letters are for! A couple of shared reading sessions, using a big book with phonetically regular text or, even better, the opportunity to decode some little phonic reading books themselves, can often have startling results in terms of children's interest in reading. But don't overdo it, because phonetically regular text is not usually very interesting, and the thrill soon wears off! The watchword in all phonics teaching should be fun!

Decoding words and non-words

In England, the phonic screening test for six-year-olds includes nonsense words, such as zarg and crinch. This is because it's important that children attend carefully to the letters when decoding an unknown word, rather than just guessing. In terms of classroom practice, however, decoding and encoding nonsense words should be a fun activity, for example in the following activity.

Words from the planet Zog

Provide a number of cards, some with real words and some with non-words written on them. Tell the children that some of the words are English ones, and some are from the planet Zog, and ask them to sort them into two piles. They can then put them in the post to send the Zoggian words back to Zog.

Supporting the development of phonic knowledge

If children are to successfully build on what they have learned in teacher-directed activities, it is essential to give careful consideration to how we can support them to tune into sound during child-initiated learning. A little thought and attention can make a massive difference.

- Make materials used for focused activities available during periods of child-initiated learning. Wherever possible, set up an area to include materials that the children can use to play the games they learned at group time. Once they know how things work, children often really enjoy playing the games by themselves.

- Make up rhymes and jingles as you work with children at play. This is much easier to do than you may think, and once you get into the habit of doing it you'll find rhymes come to you more and more easily. Such rhymes do not need to be complicated, and the children really love it when they are the subject of your rhyme. Something as simple as, *I can see Omar, walking on the balancing bar!* is quite sophisticated enough. If you make up simple rhymes consistently the children will pick up the patterns and begin to use them themselves. When jingles relate directly to the children's experience, not only do they take great delight in them, they also find them much easier to remember.

- Collect rhyming stories and poems. Rhyming texts are popular with children and great for developing phonemic awareness. The advantage of having a special collection is that you can deliberately select from it on a daily basis.

- Encourage children to take rhyming texts home. Ensure there are plenty of rhyming stories and poem books in the library box for home borrowing, including those familiar to the children through your 'five a day' reading. They will love showing off to their parents how well they know the rhymes.

- Model word building techniques, not only during shared writing, but as you take down children's words as part of their play. Model also how to decode when you and the children come across an unfamiliar word, for instance when you're out on a walk.

- Provide materials that help to develop phonemic awareness. Make sure that there are plenty of jigsaws, card games, magnetic letters, letter cutters, phonix cubes and other resources that children can use during child-initiated learning.

- Make little phonically regular books available for children to read, if they wish, during child-initiated activities – and, if they wish, to take home to share with parents. Once they are aware of sound-symbol relationships, many children find a real sense of achievement in decoding a little story all by themselves. This must be voluntary, however, as insisting that children decode before they're ready to do so is likely to be counter-productive. Make it clear – for example by storing the phonically-regular books separately – that these are not the same as 'real books'. They are teaching material, the bibliographic version of a jigsaw or card game.

- Talk with children about the sound and structure of letters and words and show excitement when they make up rhymes, play with sounds or comment on words and letters. In short, have fun with language!

Moving into writing

Writing is the most difficult of the three Rs, as it involves marshalling a wide range of concepts, skills and knowledge. Many activities suggested in previous chapters prepare children for aspects of writing:

- competence and confidence in speaking and listening, a wide vocabulary, well-developed auditory memory and access to a range of expressive language structures (Chapters 1, 2, 3)

- familiarity with the patterns of written language through frequent hearing and repeating of favourite stories (Chapter 4)

- a thorough acquaintance with the alphabet names and letters shapes (Chapter 5)

- understanding of what writing is, what it's for and how phonic knowledge is involved in converting spoken words into printed letters (see Chapters 5 and 6)

- sound phonemic awareness and a firm understanding of the main ways speech sounds are represented in writing (see Chapter 6).

One further aspect needs attention throughout the pre-school years: preparation for the task of manoeuvring a pencil across a page. In the past, too many children – especially boys – have been asked to do this fine motor task before they are physically competent to do so. This is demotivating in the extreme and likely to lead to long-term problems with writing, and perhaps literacy in general. We therefore believe strongly that the formal teaching of writing (i.e. small-scale, careful writing of letters and words) should be delayed until at least Year 1.

This is not to say that children should not learn about the letters and how to form them. But this learning should start with large-scale movements from the shoulder, which can then be refined into medium-scale movements, such as skywriting in the air using the hand and forearm, and eventually into writing with a marker pen on a small whiteboard, or a chubby pencil on paper. Plenty of practice of letter formation in this way – linked to music, dance and art – provides a secure foundation for the development of neat, fluent handwriting at a later stage.

Handwriting movements

Successful handwriting depends upon secure motor control and hand-eye coordination. For some children (especially girls) these skills seem to come fairly naturally; for others (especially boys) they are not natural at all. We have to provide opportunities for all children to succeed in handwriting, by addressing the skills at a variety of physical levels. Throughout the EYFS children need plenty of opportunities to develop:

- physical control through large-scale movement, such as outdoor play, balancing, climbing, marching and moving to music

- manipulative skills, such as using tools, cooking utensils and scissors

- fine motor control and hand-eye coordination, through activities such as jigsaws, threading, cutting, and manipulating small world equipment.

Since young children's opportunities to move freely in and around home are nowadays often severely curtailed, it's more important than ever that these opportunities are available throughout the EYFS.

There are three key movements underpinning letter formation – c (curly caterpillar), l (long ladder) and r (one-armed robot) shapes. These should be introduced through large-scale movements, from the shoulder and can be linked to music and drama, and in the earliest

stages children can make the movements symmetrically using both arms (the Write Dance programme from the Netherlands provides exciting and motivating activities of this kind). Children need considerable practice of each of the three movements at this level, to develop coordination and control, and to establish them in kinaesthetic memory.

Once a movement is firmly established, you can ask the children to try it with the right arm only, again giving plenty of opportunities to practice and 'overlearn' the shape and direction (see Appendix 6 for notes on left-handers). The next stage is to reduce the scale – for instance, skywriting with the forefinger, or mark-making with sticks in sand, squeezy bottles of water in the playground, wet sponges on a board, and so on. Finally, this shape-making can come down to an even smaller scale, in art activities using felt pens, crayons and chubby pencils.

Children who – despite many opportunities for developing gross motor control and manipulative skills – still have problems with motor control and coordination, may need special help. Early identification can make a great deal of difference, so if you are worried refer the child immediately to an educational psychologist.

Activities

Start at the caterpillar's head. Come back and round his back and curl up for his tail.

Come DOWN the long ladder and flick.

DOWN the robot's body. Up .... and over for his robot arm.

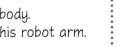

Activities such as the following develop children's confidence and fluency of movement. When possible, encourage them to make shapes using key handwriting movements:

- anti-clockwise curves (the curly caterpillar)

- straight downward strokes (down the long ladder)

- down, then up and over strokes (the one armed robot).

Fun with cous cous

You need: a builder's tray or a sand tray and a plentiful supply of uncooked cous cous.

Pour the cous cous over the bottom of the builder's tray until it is completely covered. Encourage the children to use their fingers to make marks in the grains. Show them how to make a variety of patterns in the cous cous and encourage them to use more than one finger at a time to make multiple tracks through the grains. Cut some 'combs' from some stiff card and add these to the builder's tray. Try this activity with sieved sand, rice or paint that has been applied to the bottom of the tray with a roller. When using grains, pasta and pulses give the children some tweezers with which they can grip and sort the contents of the tray. This will really help to develop fine motor control.

Design your own wallpaper

You need: Some old rolls of wallpaper, decorators' paint brushes, sawn off broom handles and some paint.

This activity is best done outdoors! Screw the paintbrushes to the broom handles and roll out the wallpaper reverse side up. Weight it down with stones if necessary. Show the children how to use the long handled brushes to make a variety of marks on the paper, and then encourage them to experiment. This activity will really encourage them to 'work from the shoulder'. Try using the brushes to paint on concrete with water and if you are feeling really adventurous, try painting on the wallpaper with soft nylon bristled sweeping brushes!

Ever increasing circles

You need: cat litter trays or similar, sugar paper, salt cellars and plenty of salt.

Line the bottom of the cat litter trays with black or dark blue sugar paper. Show the children how to fill the salt cellars and use them to make patterns. Start in the middle of the sand tray and pour the salt to make a pattern that spirals out to the edge of the tray. Encourage the children to try the same thing with a square or a rectangle shape. Let them experiment with other shapes, letters and pictures. Once they have poured all the salt from the cellar they can refill it and start again.

While some children (especially girls) have a predisposition towards fine motor skills which fits them for handwriting, they are often less naturally disposed towards gross motor movements and visuo-spatial skills. In our zeal to promote literacy skills, we should not forget to devote time helping these 'natural writers' develop physical and visuo-spatial skills that may not come naturally to them – for instance, the capacity for 'big picture thinking', judging distances, spatial awareness and whatever else it is they will one day need to do to park a car satisfactorily.

Letter formation

Children need plenty of time and practice to develop complete control of the three underpinning movements, as described on page 82, before teaching of specific letter formations begins. They should also be thoroughly familiar with the alphabet letters and their names and shapes, through activities such as making letter shapes from pastry, clay or scrunched-up foil (see page 63).

When teaching begins, the letters are best taught in groups, depending on their formation, and many children benefit from associating each letter formation with a familiar 'jingle' (see Appendix 4). On page 77, we suggest that skywriting of letters can accompany phonics teaching, but most children are ready to learn basic phonics long before they're confident about writing, so in the early stages this should be large-scale practice only (see Appendix 10).

Once the movement, direction and shape of the letters are firmly established, the scale can be reduced, as described on page 88. But in these early stages, the teaching of handwriting skills should be thought of as 'learning through movement'. If they aren't pressured to do so, most children will delight in being able to write familiar regular words for themselves. So don't rush into written phonics lessons until children are confident about writing the letters reasonably fluently – this will vary greatly from child to child (the ones who are good at phonics won't necessarily be good at handwriting, and vice versa).

Small individual whiteboards are ideal for small-scale practice. These should be blank on one side, for large-scale practice to develop fluency, but with wide lines on the reverse, as the shape, size and orientation of letters depend upon their relationship to the line (the 'jingles' in Appendix 4 refer to the line as 'the ground') – see resources list on page 136 for whiteboard supplier.

Many children, especially girls, are keen to write at an early age and their mark-making goes through well-established developmental stages – see Appendix 5. Opportunities to write during role-play allows them to develop naturally as writers (see pages 64 and 70). Once they are presented with phonic data and shown how this is used to create words, many will progress to 'real writing' just as naturally – often before you cover letter-formation with the group. Such children should not be held back, but they should be given help (individually and as necessary) to ensure they form letters correctly, or they could pile up problems for the future.

Activities

This page should be read alongside notes in Appendix 6 on left-handed children.

Demonstrating letter formation

Demonstration of letter formation requires at least two practitioners – one to stand at the front (with her back to the children) modelling the action. This might be modelling from the shoulder, in the form of skywriting. The children stand behind the modeller and mimic the actions. Any other available adults should be behind the children, watching how they get on and gently adjusting their movements as necessary.

If it is impossible to provide enough adult help, older children are often very keen to be the demonstrator(s), and it can be a useful way of helping older children with handwriting difficulties to refine their own control of the letter shapes.

Liaising with parents

Stress the importance of careful preparation for handwriting at parents' meetings before children start school, and ask parents not to push handwriting till their children seem keen and interested. However, parents should be aware of the school's handwriting style from as early as possible so they can help at home when appropriate – a handwriting sheet or booklet should be available.

Children usually want to write their names long before the teaching of writing begins in earnest, and often this is taught at home. Provide a card for each parent/carer illustrating the correct letter formation for their child's name, and ask parents to help their child form the letters correctly (and not write the whole name in capitals) – otherwise, children might overlearn incorrect movements with every signature. Give out these cards at the earliest opportunity, explaining that there's no rush to teach the signature, but when the child is ready, this is how to do it.

Letter formation jingles

Many children find it helpful to hear (and join in with) a consistent jingle to accompany the movement (see Appendix 4). The practitioner at the back of the room should take responsibility for saying the jingle, while the demonstrator at the front, like the children, moves in response to it. This means the jingle-speaker can, in the early stages, read the words of the jingle, ensuring they're consistent. As time goes on, the children should become familiar enough with the words to join in.

Writing the letters

Once children are familiar with the letter-shapes and able to make the movements fluently, you can transfer to smaller-scale practice, for instance using

- **paper on easels with stubby crayons or marker pens**
- **mini-whiteboards and large marker pens.**

By this point, it is possible to link letter-formation practice to phonics revision, and we recommend addressing the letters in the groups shown in Appendix 4. Children will continue to need frequent and regular demonstration of letter formation, and this should always be done by a practitioner with her back to the class, so children do not see hand-movements in reverse.

Rebecca

The handwriting font illustrated above was developed by handwriting expert Rosemary Sassoon. The letter formation is simple and clear, and leads easily into a joined script as soon as appropriate.

Pencil control

Holding a pencil puts strain on the thumb and first two fingers of the writing hand. If children are asked to write at any length before these muscles are strong enough for comfortable manipulation of the pencil, the act of writing can be physically painful. We believe that many children, especially boys, are put off writing from the very start because of these painful associations. In any good early years setting there will be numerous resources that will help to strengthen the children's finger muscles as they work with them, but some experiences are better than others – see opposite.

There should also be opportunities for children to use crayons, marker pens, and chubby pencils, for example:

* drawing, tracing (not handwriting worksheets!), colouring

* emergent writing in role-play situations, using chubby pencils, crayons or marker pens

* phonics activities, using individual whiteboards and marker pens – children write individual letters and consonant-vowel-consonant (CVC) (or later CCVC/CVCC) words in response to the teacher's dictation.

When they are writing, tracing or drawing, help children develop an effective pencil grip. The sooner you intervene to stop them grasping the pencil incorrectly, the less likely they are to overlearn an awkward grip. If they find it difficult to adjust their grip, place the pencil appropriately between their fingers and lightly guide their hand as they draw or trace. Keep the activity light-hearted, praise them immoderately for correct pencil grip, and make light of any regressions – just keep making gentle adjustments.

Pencil grip for a right-handed child.

Activities

The finger muscles can be strengthened through many activities – but it's important to ensure there is a range of appropriate materials, so that all children have frequent opportunities to exercise these muscles, no matter what their interests.

Creative activities

- painting with fingers and with a wide variety of paintbrushes

- manipulating malleable materials for example dough, Plasticine, clay, that can be pounded, rolled, moulded and pinched

- working creatively with scissors, staplers, hole punches, treasury tags, recycled materials etc.

- sprinkling sand and glitter in the creative area

- mark-making in a well-equipped mark-making area (see page 76).

Sorting and sequencing

- picking up and sorting, with fingers or tweezers, collections of pulses, pasta, beads and sequins

- sorting or sequencing items with pegs on a washing line, for example socks, clothes, number, picture or letter cards (this can be done indoors or out).

Building and making

- using woodwork tools such as screwdrivers, hammers and pliers

- playing with commercial construction equipment, for example stickle bricks, popoids, brio, mini quadro, interstar, polydrons etc.

- manipulating clay or Plasticine to create models (Plasticine is better than playdough because it requires more muscular effort to manipulate)

- weaving, sewing and threading (a bicycle wheel mounted on an outside wall is excellent for large-scale weaving, alternatively, provide a box of ribbon and fabric and make use of the railings!)

- when working with food (or pretend food), using garlic presses, cutters and icing bags.

Activities

Play equipment

- collections of nuts and bolts, locks and keys
- a range of finger puppets
- a good selection of jigsaws
- pegboards in a variety of sizes.

Finger rhymes

As well as *Incy Wincy Spider* there are many rhymes involving finger-play, for example:

Here's the church
Here's the church and here's the steeple
Open the door and here's all the people
First they sing and then they pray
And then they quietly walk away.

Daily routines

- helping to prepare fruit and vegetables for snack times
- putting on and buttoning or zipping coats and other clothes
- tying bows (for example shoelaces, ribbons, ties on aprons).
- Ask children who are competent at these skills to help their peers who are still struggling.

There are a variety of commercial pencil grips and triangular pencils available, to help develop pencil grip.

Shared writing

In Chapter 5 we recommend regular shared writing as a way of gradually helping children to:

- understand the purposes of writing
- assimilate the relevant vocabulary and the main principles of composition and transcription.

In Nursery, shared writing will generally arise informally within child-initiated activities, but a short group session relating to the ongoing life of the classroom could happen perhaps once a week. It should be a kind of 'pole-bridged composition' with the emphasis on converting meaning into words or, sometimes, short sentences.

By the end of Reception, shared writing with the whole group should be almost a daily activity, involving oral rehearsal of each sentence before writing, and sometimes talk about where to start writing, why we leave spaces between words, etc. The practitioner should model how to constantly re-read what's already been written to maintain the sense. Such sessions should not, however, take more than about 15 minutes. In Chapter 6 we also suggest that, once phonic work has begun, the practitioner can occasionally take the opportunity during shared writing to show how phonic knowledge is used, but never to the extent that emphasis on encoding distracts from the overall meaning.

Shared writing thus becomes a key element in helping children understand the intrinsic nature of composition, and the way all the constituent skills must be orchestrated to put meaning down on paper. At all stages, children should also be encouraged to compose their own sentences and stories, but they do not need to write them down: saying them to a partner or reporting them to the class will be enough. Written composition, involving the orchestration of all the skills outlined on page 81, should wait until all the foundations of literacy, including letter formation and pencil control, are in place.

Activities

The secret of successful shared writing is to integrate it into the ongoing life of the setting. Use the many 'real' writing opportunities that crop up as a way of demonstrating the significance and importance of the written word – and the many ways it helps us in day-to-day life. Do make sure, however, that you never go on too long. If the shared writing task is a long one, choose which section you will demonstrate, and write the rest at some other time. You might have the start of a letter written up before the shared session, so you can read it to the children and ask them to help you finish it. Or you might write the start of a story and promise to finish it (to the children's design) while they're playing – then you can read the whole thing to them later in the day.

Cards and invitations

Most children's earliest encounters with writing are through birthday and Christmas cards, and party invitations. Take opportunities to model how these are written, for example:

- show how to compose an invitation to a party in the setting (for example a teddy bears picnic), which you can then print to hand out to each child

- show how to make birthday or Christmas cards to 'our story' characters (see page 52) or to characters in books

- use shared writing to demonstrate how to write Love + signature in Mother's Day cards, etc. when the children are making cards to send home.

Letters, postcards and emails

Use shared writing to compose letters home to give information (you need only model a small part of the letter), or ask children to help you compose a postcard, letter or email to a classmate on long term absence from school.

Notices and labels for the setting

When you need a new label or sign to be placed around the setting, compose and write it during a shared writing session. Ask pupils to help you find the most appropriate wording. This is a perfect opportunity to demonstrate the importance and consistency of print, as children will then see your writing displayed in context in the setting – and these writing opportunities arise on a regular basis.

Lists, lists, lists

Whenever shopping is required – for parties, for cooking activities, when replenishing any sort of stocks – ask the children to help you compose the list. Similarly, ask children to help you make 'To do' lists for yourself and for them. Or make lists of children's favourite things: favourite animals, foods, books, television characters, and so on.

Poems

Compose poems on experiences or topics of interest (children suggest ideas, words, lines and you scribe them). As you write them down, you can model how to decide when to start a new line, how to keep changing and improving the poem, etc.

Stories and books

When you engage in storytelling activities, as described in Chapter 4, some stories will emerge which become children's favourites. These stories cry out to be written down and illustrated. Do some of the writing as a shared writing activity (not all, as this could get boring), and invite children to provide illustrations to make your own book (either homemade, or using pages stuck in a scrap-books).

Rules and regulations

Use shared writing whenever you and the children need to discuss issues of behaviour. If you involve the children in discussing why things go wrong, how they can be solved, and devising rules to make the life of the setting go more smoothly, they are more likely to remember and abide by those rules. And as they compose them, you can write them out for future display.

Supporting emergent writing

If children are to begin to see themselves as writers it is essential that we provide them with opportunities to role-play and to make marks and representations on paper.

Encourage mark-making

- provide plenty of opportunities for mark-making outside (playground chalks, blackboards mounted on the wall, painting with water etc.)

- provide mark-making equipment and large paper in the small world area so that children can make their own play mats

- encourage children to put as much detail as possible into their drawings (note that drawing is first-draft writing, and children who are still drawing figures where the arms and legs emanate from the head are not ready to begin forming letters!)

- provide a writing area (see below).

Facilitate 'literate' role-play

- resource the home corner with materials for children to make shopping lists, write messages, list jobs to be done, write notes for the milkman etc

- help children to make pretend registers

- encourage them to make badges, tickets and money as part of their play

- encourage them to write signs and labels as part of their play, for example 'The shop is open'

- in restaurant play areas, help them make menus and price lists and model how to take orders.

Encouraging written communication

- encourage them to write instructions, for example 'This way to the sand'

- support them to write letters and make cards for parents, friends and family members

- provide message boards, post boxes and pigeon holes, and model how to use them.

Providing reasons for writing

- encourage children to 'sign up' for child-initiated activities

- write notices to which the children can make a response, for example 'Who has made some cakes today? Sign here!'

- provide clipboards in the construction and workshop areas so that children can record their ideas.

Always have a writing corner

- Resources for the writing corner will to some extent depend on the amount of space available, but some must be regarded as essential:

- paper in assorted colours, sizes and shapes (paper cut in the shape of vehicles, dinosaurs and space rockets is useful for attracting boys to the area)

- stationary and envelopes

- pens, pencils, felt tip pens, crayons etc.

- scissors, stapler, hole punch, treasury tags and Sellotape

- message board, post box, pigeon holes, telephone and note pads

- alphabet chart with examples of upper and lower case letters

- clipboards (buy A5 clipboards which are much easier for young children to handle)

- name card for each of the children

- Where space permits the following resources are also highly desirable: labels - calendars - date stamp – glue sticks - greetings cards - rulers - rubbers - address books - diaries - pencil sharpeners - typewriter - files - paper clips – bulldog clips - postcards - assorted ready-made books - split pins - calculator - pinboard - elastic bands - simple dictionaries.

Sound foundations

We have described seven strands of early learning which we consider essential before formal teaching of literacy begins. By 'formal teaching', we mean activities such as:

- whole-class literacy instruction, for example in phonics, spelling or handwriting

- working through a structured reading scheme

- requiring children to write down stories, 'news', etc. on a regular basis.

The sorts of adult-directed activities described in *Foundations of Literacy* are essentially playful, and designed to work alongside and blend in with children's self-initiated play. They're informed by the long-established principle that play is children's natural development drive, and that between the ages of three and six the best way to provide sound foundations for literacy (or any academic learning) is to respect and support that innate drive.

Attention to each *Foundations of Literacy* strand, supporting children's implicit learning of the concepts and skills underpinning literacy, is more likely to lead to confidence and eventual success than early formal teaching. By the age of six, most children should have reached a level of emotional, social, physical and cognitive development at which they are able consciously to control their own behaviour and thought processes. At this point, they are ready for more formal, explicit teaching of literacy skills.

The capacity to read and write does not come naturally to human beings. It involves conscious knowledge about the way text is constructed (see diagram below) and conscious physical control of complex motor movements. Formal, explicit teaching of literacy skills involves helping children develop this knowledge and control, then providing sufficient practice of decoding and encoding text to automatise the processes of reading and writing. It is arguably the single most important element of primary education, and is much more likely to be successful if children begin school with sound developmental foundations in place (see bulleted text in the diagram).

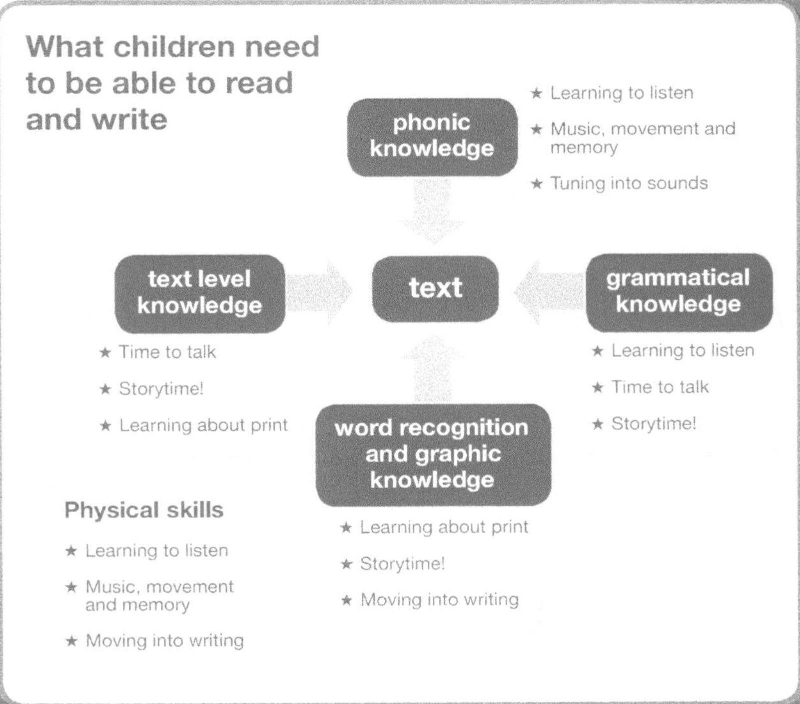

What children need to be able to read and write

phonic knowledge
- ★ Learning to listen
- ★ Music, movement and memory
- ★ Tuning into sounds

text level knowledge
- ★ Time to talk
- ★ Storytime!
- ★ Learning about print

text

grammatical knowledge
- ★ Learning to listen
- ★ Time to talk
- ★ Storytime!

word recognition and graphic knowledge
- ★ Learning about print
- ★ Storytime!
- ★ Moving into writing

Physical skills
- ★ Learning to listen
- ★ Music, movement and memory
- ★ Moving into writing

The Foundations of Literacy 'curriculum'

The *Foundations of Literacy* curriculum is designed for children between the ages of three and six. At each stage, it includes all seven strands of practice, but the emphasis changes as children grow older. In the early stages, practitioners will be concentrating on the development of listening and language skills in general; by the later stages, there is more specific emphasis on the skills underpinning reading and writing.

In the same way, there will be a gradual change in the balance of adult-initiated and child-initiated activities throughout the three years. It is not easy to orchestrate a daily routine where this balance perfectly matches the developmental needs of the children, as the relationship between the two aspects of learning is a dynamic one, requiring great responsiveness from practitioners. Generally speaking, the younger the child, the more

Foundations of Literacy activities should be woven seamlessly into the fabric of the daily routine. The suggestions on pages 98-99 for integrating *Foundations of Literacy* throughout the day's activities are aimed at four- to five-year-old children (in England, the Reception class), but the basic principles hold good for the entire age range. For younger children, timings will probably be slightly shorter, for older children there will be more emphasis on adult-directed activities, although child-initiated activities are still important.

At every stage, *Foundations of Literacy* is consistent with the best pre-school practice. On pages 95-96, we show how it overlaps with the requirements of the EYFS in England. The practitioners in our trialling schools have found this type of cross-referencing helpful in planning the work of the setting.

Foundations of Literacy curriculum for three- to four-year-olds

Listening:

daily activities to improve discrimination, develop social listening skills

increase attention span, develop auditory memory (overlap with music and storytime)

Talk:

daily spoken language activities, including repeating and innovating on sentences (circle time), targeting selected vocabulary and PREPARE expressive language; activities to compensate for language delay

Music/Memory

daily opportunities to keep a steady beat, sing (and learn) songs, action songs and rhymes; frequent opportunities to move rhythmically (for example marching, dancing)

Storytime

five a day' reading of storybooks; frequent storytelling sessions; regular opportunities for children to make up stories

Print

frequent attention to environmental print through walks, in classroom, in role-play areas; frequent singing of alphabet song, linked to chart and activities with letters; demonstration of different types of reading

Phonics

daily rhyme, rhythm and song (link to music); daily rhyming activities

Writing

activities to develop gross, medium and fine motor skills; large-scale handwriting movement activities (link to music, drama, art); attention to pencil grip; occasional relevant shared writing

Foundations of Literacy curriculum for four- to five-year-olds

Listening:

daily activities to improve discrimination, develop social listening skills, increase attention span, develop auditory memory (overlap with music and storytime, phonics); weekly learning of a simple rhyme

Talk:

daily spoken language activities, including repeating and innovating on sentences (circle time), targeting selected vocabulary and PREPARE expressive language; activities to compensate for language delay

Music/Memory

regular opportunities to develop rhythm, sing (and learn) songs, action songs and rhymes; frequent opportunities to move rhythmically (for example marching, dancing)

Storytime

'five a day' reading of stories; frequent storytelling sessions; regular opportunities to make up stories

Print

frequent attention to environmental print: gradual linking of alphabet knowledge to phonics; demonstration of different types of reading

Phonics

daily rhyme, rhythm and song (link to music); daily oral activities to learn phonemes and to segment and blend; later, daily phonic activities, using magnetic letters; integration of phonic knowledge into shared writing

Writing

large-scale letter formation (link to music, drama, art); frequent large-scale practice of letter formation; attention to pencil grip and handedness; daily shared writing

Foundations of Literacy curriculum for five- to six-year-olds

Listening

daily activities to develop attention span and auditory memory (overlap with music and storytime, phonics); weekly learning of a simple rhyme

Talk

daily spoken language activities, including repeating and innovating on sentences (circle time and storytime), targeting of selected vocabulary and PREPARE expressive language; activities to compensate for language delay

Music/Memory

regular opportunities to develop rhythm, sing (and learn) songs, action songs and rhymes; frequent opportunities to move rhythmically (for example marching, dancing)

Storytime

'five a day' reading of storybooks and frequent storytelling sessions, with emphasis on children's retelling of stories; regular opportunities for children to make up stories

Print

frequent attention to environmental print; gradual linking of alphabet knowledge to phonics; demonstration of different types of reading; sight word activities

Phonics

daily rhyme, rhythm and song (link to music); daily phonic activities, using magnetic letters, etc. and linking to letter-formation; reading, when children are ready, of phonically-regular material; integration of phonic knowledge into shared writing

Writing

frequent practice of letter formation; attention to pencil grip and handedness; daily shared writing

Fitting it in

The guidance for the EYFS in England clearly states that the best possible daily routine for three-, four- and five-year-olds involves an appropriate balance between adult-initiated and child-initiated activities. For young children, learning cannot be compartmentalized, so practitioners need to be highly skilled at ensuring that the foundations for literacy are built into every aspect of the daily routine.

In order to do this effectively, we suggest practitioners plan for children's learning on a term-by-term, week-by-week, day-by-day and hour-by-hour basis, paying close attention to how the seven strands of the curriculum are woven throughout the day's activities and across the areas of learning. As many opportunities arise in response to the children's current interests and motivations, and are therefore difficult to plan for, practitioners should carry out regular audits (see Appendices 7-9).

All settings are different and necessarily manage time, space, people and the daily routine in ways that best suit their individual needs. However, there are elements that are common to all settings, and the list of elements of a Reception day given on pages 98-99 give examples of how the *Foundations of Literacy* curriculum can be woven throughout these elements. Although this list was originally devised for four- to five-year-olds, the elements do not differ greatly from those found in a Nursery setting or the first term of a Year 1 class. In the Nursery setting adult-directed activities will probably be shorter and simpler, while throughout the course of Reception and Year 1 they will become increasingly complex and extended, as the children become more able to concentrate on an adult agenda.

Activities

Welcome time (10–15 minutes)

This provides opportunities for many types of *Foundations of Literacy* behaviour, for example adults model respectful listening as they greet children and parents; practitioners, children and parents converse and chat; children use their name cards to self register; adults and children use the message board to note down things that are important to remember and relevant to the day; children sing a song, make up a rap or finger rhyme as others arrive; children select books and activities with which to work until welcome time is over.

Snack time (10–15 minutes)

This part of the daily routine provides many opportunities for social language and listening.

Planning for periods of child-initiated learning (5–10 minutes)

When children are thinking about and planning for how they will spend their time, there are opportunities for them to share their plans in pairs; see their ideas being written down by an adult; make up raps about who is going to do what; speak their plans into a microphone or hand-held recording device; draw and talk about their plans.

Child-initiated learning (at least 45 minutes)

As children work at their own self-directed activities, you can listen, talk, use rhyme, make music, role-play with and write for them. All this should be done in a way that complements and does not interrupt their play. It helps to make posters of the key elements of the *Foundations of Literacy* curriculum (for example see Appendices 7-9) and put them around the setting as a memory aid. After a while, the process will become so second nature that you will not need to refer to the posters at all.

Focused activity time (10–20 minutes)

The length of focused activity time varies, depending on children's developmental level. When it has a Communication and Language focus, it could involve listening games; circle time activities; role-play activities; phonic games; print based activities; steady beat sessions; shared writing; gross motor activities outside; focused time in the mark-making area; handwriting activities involving music, movement, drama and art. When the focus revolves around another area of the learning, there may still be opportunities for literacy development (see pages 119-133).

Tidy up time (5–10 minutes)

Tidy up time offers opportunities for singing, rhyming, rapping and musical activities. You can play music with a strong beat as a background to the whole process, or play marching music and march from one place to another as you put things away.

Review time/Plenary
(10 minutes)

The opportunities at planning time are again available during review of child-initiated learning.

Whole-class activities
(approximately 15 minutes)

The opportunity for children to meet in a large group might involve: stories (several short books can be read within one session); circle time activities (talk and listening); action rhymes and songs; listening games; shared writing activities; steady beat, rhythm, music and movement activities.

Transition times

As each part of the daily routine comes to an end and gives way to a new activity, you can use a rap, rhyme or song that relates to what you have just done or something you are about to become involved in. Marching from one place to another helps develop basic timing!

Story and home time
(10–15 minutes)

Preparing for the end of the day is a further opportunity to gather for stories and song. If there are letters to be given out, talk about their purpose with the children and where appropriate, encourage them to ask questions about their content.

Creating the culture

On page 94 and in the audit sheets in Appendices 7–9, we outline the elements of the *Foundations of Literacy* curriculum relevant for children at different stages between the ages of three and six. However, the experience children bring to a setting varies greatly, so there may be a wide range of ability. Some children will find *Foundations of Literacy* activities relatively easy; others may find them challenging and need plenty of one-to-one help and encouragement. Some groups may, on the whole, be able to move rapidly through the programme; others will need gradual, incremental encouragement, with plenty of consolidation at each stage. Practitioners must use their own experience and expertise to assess the speed with which to proceed.

However, we believe the key element in creating the *Foundations of Literacy* culture is to value the skills of speaking and listening. For far too long these have been taken for granted in British settings and schools, and their huge importance in all learning has simply not been recognized. We believe this is the main reason for our difficulties in raising literacy standards, especially among those children who do not come from 'language-rich' backgrounds. Our educational ethos requires us to press on with literacy skills at the earliest possible opportunity, and the whole of our national culture reflects this ethos. It's therefore extremely important that we explain

Foundations of Literacy clearly to parents, so they do not fear we are 'holding their children back'.

Elsewhere in Europe, spoken language activities are a valued part of education throughout children's school careers. What's more, the two countries which, in international studies, have the greatest success in literacy – Sweden and Finland – have a completely oral curriculum until children are seven years old. Here in the UK, we must get away from the idea that sitting silently 'on the mat' staring at an electronic whiteboard, ploughing at an early age through a reading scheme, or struggling to write a story when they can hardly hold a pencil are somehow 'good for children'.

The seven strands of *Foundations of Literacy* – with their constant emphasis on speaking and listening – not only provide the building blocks for literacy so that, once formal teaching begins, more children succeed and fewer fail. They also focus on the enjoyment and appreciation of literacy, so that children want to read and write, and will thus develop their literacy skills through willing practice. Perhaps most important of all, they provide the basis of an essential life-skill which we ignore at our peril – the ability to explore and express our ideas through language, and to communicate our needs and feelings to others. It is the development of these skills, in all our citizens, upon which society ultimately depends.

Activities

The finger muscles can be strengthened through many activities – but it's important to ensure there is a range of appropriate materials, so that all children have frequent opportunities to exercise these muscles, no matter what their interests.

Little by little

When introducing *Foundations of Literacy*, don't try to do everything at once. Focus on each strand of the *Foundations of Literacy* curriculum in turn and consider how it can be developed in your setting through each aspect of the daily routine (see page 81). Focus on a strand for one week, becoming aware of what works well and what doesn't. Once you have been through this process you will be in a position to do more of what works on purpose! Then move on to consider another strand of *Foundations of Literacy* in the same systematic way until you have covered all of them. When you have done this, use the appropriate audit sheet (see pages 112 – 114) on a weekly basis to check out that all strands of the curriculum are receiving sufficient attention. Once you are clear that everything is receiving systematic attention you will need to audit less often.

It's good to talk

Teach conflict resolution. When young children are in conflict over space, materials or friends, teach them how to:

- acknowledge their feelings in a difficult situation

- gather information by re-stating what has happened

- generate possible solutions and choose one together (and once they have done this, make sure you offer any necessary follow-up support).

As well as developing language and social skills, this helps children see – in the most meaningful of contexts – that speaking and listening are extraordinarily useful on a day-to-day basis. It's not overstating the case to say that the ability to resolve conflicts in this way underlies the institutions of our democratic system. Go for it!

Little and often

Children in the Nursery phase of early education need very short sessions of adult-initiated activities, increasing in length as their concentration spans develop. These short sessions should be spread throughout the day (see page 81). As they grow older, children should be able to maintain attention during adult-initiated activities for longer, but practitioners should always be alert to the group's attention. If you feel you've lost them, there's no point in continuing with an activity. Try something else (a song or action rhyme) and see if it revives concentration. If not, don't go on flogging the dead horse a moment longer – whatever you're doing clearly doesn't work and you need to rethink!

Sitting and moving

Small children cannot sit still for long, and many adult-initiated activities involve a certain amount of sitting 'on the mat'. As suggested above, it's important that relatively passive activities are interwoven with more active ones – for example during an adult-directed session, once you've finished a circle time sentence-completion activity, ask children to stand up for some music and movement. However, research suggests that, during circle time and other talk-based group work, children find it easier to concentrate if they are sitting on small chairs, rather than 'on the mat'. Is there any way, within your setting, of providing both comfortable seating and room to move during adult-initiated sessions?

On location

Go 'on location' as often as possible, by conducting adult-initiated sessions in the role-play area, water area, sand area, creative area, outside area etc. This enables you to model the types of play and language that are possible and appropriate, and once children are aware of the possibilities, they will return during periods of child-initiated learning and build on what you have modelled. Pay careful attention to how your team is developing children's language during play (see Chapter 2 Time to talk).

Smooth transitions

It is difficult to specify exactly when 'formal' literacy should begin. For some groups of children – for instance, children from language-rich backgrounds where many of the activities we describe are familiar before they enter school – the majority may well be secure in all seven strands by the end of the Reception year. For others, it may be that another full year should be devoted to the *Foundations of Literacy* curriculum, and formal literacy should not begin until some time in Year 2. Our feeling is that most children would benefit from following the sort of course we have described until they are at least six years old. In England, that would probably be the beginning of Year 1 Term 2. A good starting point in that term might be to use the Early Learning Support materials as a 'fast track' programme into formal literacy learning for everyone.

Whenever the transition occurs, it needs to be treated as a whole-school issue so that senior managers and the rest of the staff understand and give their support to the process. There should also be careful consideration to sharing this process with parents, who must also understand why you are doing things in the way you have agreed.

Initially, when children move from the EYFS to the National Curriculum, both the physical environment and the daily routine should mirror what children have experienced during the EYFS to the greatest possible extent. Key Stage 1 children still need access to a quality play curriculum and will develop literacy skills far more effectively when this is present. But they need more challenging resources, more complex problems to tussle with, and they need to develop more sophisticated language with which to explore their ideas.

> Some children in any group will, of course, start reading and writing before they are six through their own emergent literacy activities. They should be encouraged, their efforts celebrated, and individual help provided (for example to ensure letters are correctly formed, by linking to what you're doing in the Moving into writing strand) where necessary. These children can then form a 'top group' once formal learning starts. But in the meantime they too will benefit from a whole-class emphasis on speaking, listening, music, and social skills, along with a more informal approach to their interest in reading and writing.

This is why we recommend making the transition during the course of Year 1, so that a familiar teacher helps them move from one type of practice to another, with the minimum of 'culture shock'. The secret of success lies in beginning with what they know and are confident with, and then by a gradual process, building on those opportunities to increase the level of challenge and complexity. As Year 1 progresses, teachers should ask themselves:

- do we currently make the best possible use of the role-play area, construction materials and small world resources etc?

- have we extended periods of adult-initiated learning as the year progresses?

- do we nevertheless still support children working on their own self-initiated activities?

- do we promote independent learning so that children become skilled at using a task board and taking responsibility for their own learning?

- do we involve the children in decisions about how the classroom is organized and share responsibility for its smooth running?

- do we integrate plenty of movement -- including movement to music -- into the daily routine (especially important if you are working in a small classroom with restricted space)?

- are there any ways of recruiting more adult help into the classroom, for example by training some NVQ students, appealing to parents, friends and grandparents?

- are all areas of the *Foundations of Literacy* curriculum still receiving appropriate attention (see audit sheet on Appendix 9)?

Language development: **Normal development of expressive language**

Approximate age	Type of talk	Examples
0 –1 (the first year)	• babble • early attempts at words	*Dada*
1 – 2 (the second year)	• more recognizable words • lots of repeated words • sometimes puts two words together uses question intonation • by 18 months, knows up to 50 words, by 2 up to 200 puts two to three words together in short sentences • starts using question words	*Bye-bye* *Oggy-oggy* *Daddy there?* words for actions, food, body parts, clothes, animals, vehicles, places, pronouns, colour, shape *That my house* *What that noise?*
2 – 3 (the third year)	• puts three/four/ more word sentences together • uses word endings, for example plurals, tense • possibly 500 words by 2½; 1,000 by 3 • period of intense questioning • use of *and* to link ideas	*Me got lotsa cars like Tom.* *Daddy comed to see me in the garden.* *Why? Why? Why?* *I want juice **and** bikky!*
3 – 4 (the fourth year)	• produces increasingly long sentences • little words like *to* and *the* appear • links ideas using, for example *when*, *cos*, *after*, *before* • uses language for a variety of reasons, including: retelling favourite stories; role-play and 'pretend', • recounting events • vocabulary of up to 5000 words?	*We wented to town and we did have a haircut and then we got a Big Mac.* *I go now cos my mummy's here.* *I eated it when I watched the telly.* *You be the baby and I'll be the mummy. You sit here and I'll go and get your juice. Be good or you won't get no juice.*

Language development: Normal development of articulation

Approximate age	Consonant sounds	Speech
9 months–2 years	*m,n,* *p, b, t, d* *w* *(k, g)*	• repeated syllables, for example *Dada* • final sounds missed off words, for example *do* for *dog* • recognizable words, for example *tat* for *cat* • *k* and *g* not used all the time
2 years–3 years	*ng* *k, g* *(f, s)* *h*	• final sounds still sometimes omitted, for example *Go to tea-tie (sea-side)* • *f* and *s* sometimes used
3 years–4 years	*f, s* *v, z* *sh, ch, j* *l*	• words usually have final sound, but not always the adult one, for example *fiss* for fish • *sh*, *ch*, *j* develop later • where there are two consonants together, the child may only use one, for example *no* for *snow*
4/5 years onward	*(th, r, zh)*	• Some children have trouble with these sounds until they are around 7 years old
7 years onwards	Mature pronunciation of most words	

PREPARE chart

Plan	*Let's think about what we/you are going to do.* *What will you need?* *Tell me how you'll start.* *What will you do next?*	Thinking ahead. Sorting out sequence. *First, Next, Then..*, etc.
Recount	*Can you remember what happened when...?* *Where were you?* *Tell me how it all started.* *What happened next?* *How did it all end?*	Thinking back. Working out sequence. *In the beginning...*
Explore	*I wonder what this is?* *What might that be for?* *I wonder how it works?* *Where do you think this should go?*	Considering possibility in the here and now. Tentativeness: *I think...; Maybe*
Predict	*I wonder what's going to happen?* *Can you guess what will happen next?* *What do you think would happen if...?* *(or if we didn't...)*	Anticipating the future based on what you know. Tentativeness.
Analyse	*Gosh – what's going on here?* *Can you work out how this happened?* *Do you notice anything about...?* *Why do you think it happened?* *How did you feel when...?*	Consciousness of observation. Curiosity. Reflection on feelings.
Report	*Tell me about... What is it for?* *What does it do?* *colour/shape/size is it?* *What does it look/sound/feel/taste/smell like?*	Observation and explicitness; awareness of key features.
Explain	*Do you know how this works?* *I wonder why that happen?* *What starts it off?* *Do you know what know the reason for...?* *How do we know that?*	Curiosity: how and why? Awareness of cause and effect. Awareness of sequence.

Foundations of Literacy © Sue Palmer, Featherstone Education

The phonemes of English

Consonant phonemes with consistent spellings

/b/ **b**at, ra**bb**it

/d/ **d**og, da**dd**y

/g/ **g**irl, gi**gg**le

/h/ **h**ot

/l/ **l**og, lo**ll**y

/m/ **m**at, su**mm**er

/n/ **n**ut, di**nn**er

/p/ **p**ig, su**pp**er

/r/ **r**at, ca**rr**y

/t/ **t**op, pa**tt**er

/y/ **y**ellow

/th/ **th**is (voiced) **th**ing (unvoiced)

Consonant phonemes with alternative spellings

/k/ **c**at, **k**ing, ba**ck**, s**ch**ool, **qu**een
(also the /k/ sound in bo**x**)

/s/ **s**un, pre**ss**, **c**ircle

/f/ **f**un, **ph**oto

/j/ **j**am, **g**inger, bri**dge**

/w/ **w**orm, q**u**een

/z/ **z**oo, pin**s**, **x**ylophone

/v/ **v**an (one exception: o**f**)

/sh/ **sh**eep, sta**ti**on, **ch**ef

/ch/ **ch**in, it**ch**

/ng/ si**ng**, pi**n**k

/zh/ mea**s**ure, a**z**ure

'Short' and 'long' vowel phonemes

/a/ b**a**g

/e/ b**e**t, br**ea**d, s**ai**d

/i/ b**i**g, c**y**linder

/o/ t**o**p, w**a**s

/u/ b**u**n, l**o**ve

/ae/ d**ay**, p**ai**n, g**a**te, gr**ea**t

/ee/ f**ee**t, s**ea**t, P**e**te, m**e**

/ie/ t**ie**, t**igh**t, fl**y**, t**i**me

/oa/ b**oa**t, gr**ow**, b**o**ne, t**oe**, g**o**

/ue/ bl**ue**, m**oo**n, gr**ew**, fl**u**te, y**ou**

Other vowel phonemes

/oo/ g**oo**d, p**u**t, c**ou**ld, w**o**lf

/ur/ ch**ur**ch, b**ir**d, h**er**b, **ear**th, w**or**d

/ar/ st**ar**t, f**a**ther

/or/ c**or**n, d**oo**r, sh**o**re, r**oar**, y**our**
p**aw**, t**au**t, t**a**ll, t**a**lk, t**augh**t

/ow/ cl**ow**n, sh**ou**t

/oy/ b**oy**, **oi**l

/ear/ n**ear**, d**ee**r, h**ere**

/air/ ch**air**, sh**are**, th**ere**

/ure/ p**ure**, t**our**ist

'schwa' (an indeterminate 'uh' sound)
farm**er**, doct**or**, gramm**ar**, met**re**, col**our**, Americ**a**.....

First ensure children can hear and imitate the phoneme, then introduce one way of writing it (i.e. the first spelling pattern given in each list of examples). Other main spelling patterns can be introduced, as required, widening the spelling choices.

Foundations of Literacy © Sue Palmer, Featherstone Education

Handwriting groups and jingles

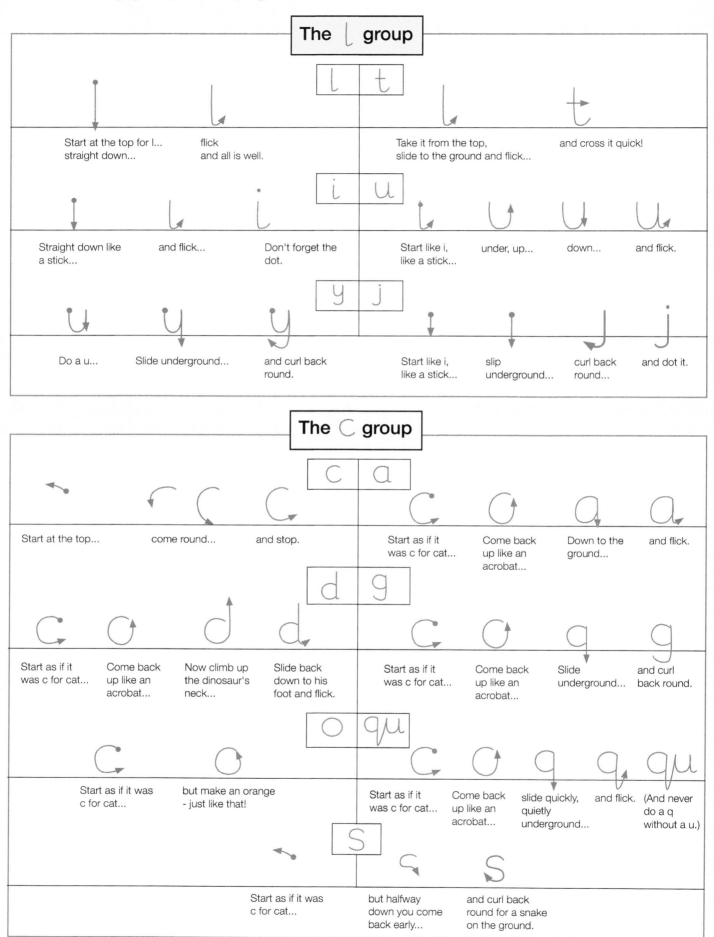

The l group

l t

Start at the top for l... straight down...   flick and all is well.

Take it from the top, slide to the ground and flick...   and cross it quick!

i u

Straight down like a stick...   and flick...   Don't forget the dot.

Start like i, like a stick...   under, up...   down...   and flick.

y j

Do a u...   Slide underground...   and curl back round.

Start like i, like a stick...   slip underground...   curl back round...   and dot it.

The c group

c a

Start at the top...   come round...   and stop.

Start as if it was c for cat...   Come back up like an acrobat...   Down to the ground...   and flick.

d g

Start as if it was c for cat...   Come back up like an acrobat...   Now climb up the dinosaur's neck...   Slide back down to his foot and flick.

Start as if it was c for cat...   Come back up like an acrobat...   Slide underground...   and curl back round.

o qu

Start as if it was c for cat...   but make an orange - just like that!

Start as if it was c for cat...   Come back up like an acrobat...   slide quickly, quietly underground...   and flick.   (And never do a q without a u.)

s

Start as if it was c for cat...   but halfway down you come back early...   and curl back round for a snake on the ground.

The r group

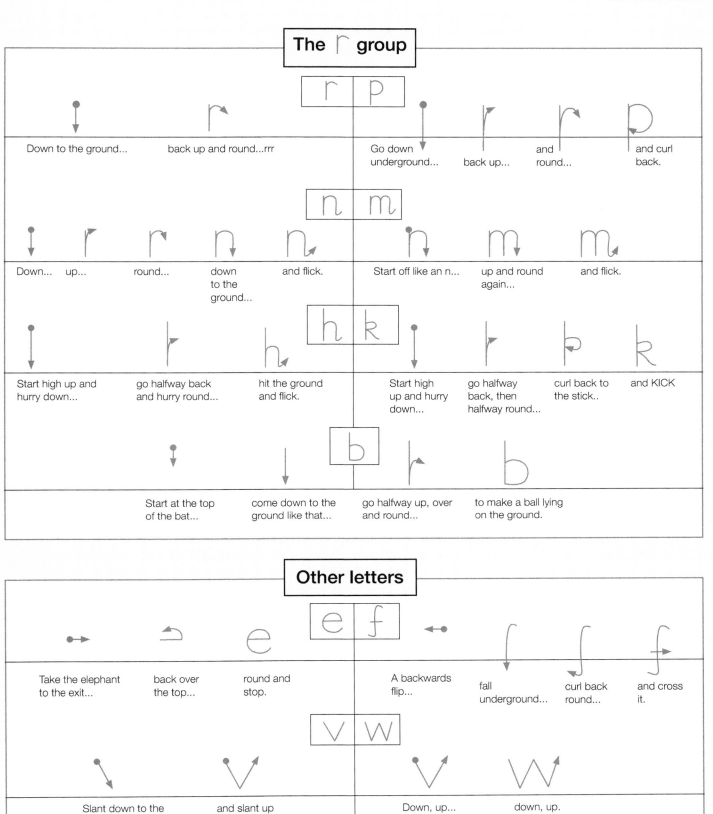

Down to the ground... back up and round...rrr

Go down underground... back up... and round... and curl back.

Down... up... round... down to the ground... and flick.

Start off like an n... up and round again... and flick.

Start high up and hurry down... go halfway back and hurry round... hit the ground and flick.

Start high up and hurry down... go halfway back, then halfway round... curl back to the stick.. and KICK

Start at the top of the bat... come down to the ground like that... go halfway up, over and round... to make a ball lying on the ground.

Other letters

Take the elephant to the exit... back over the top... round and stop.

A backwards flip... fall underground... curl back round... and cross it.

Slant down to the ground... and slant up in the air...

Down, up... down, up.

Slant down to the ground... lift your pen... up in the air... cross back again.

Zoom forward... zig zag back... zoom again.

Stages in emergent writing

This developmental checklist, taken from the National Literacy Strategy materials for teaching assistants (2000), provides a guide to the normal developmental progression of handwriting and phonic skills in children's emergent writing. Progress will be accelerated if practitioners provide pointers and models (through the type of commentary chosen during shared writing and individual help during child-initiated learning) of the next stage:

- Random scribble

- Scribble that looks like writing

- Individual shapes that look like letters

- Some real letters used randomly (especially letters from own name)

- Letters and shapes written from left to right across the page

- Individual letters used to represent words (usually initial sounds)

- More than one letter used to represent a word (usually significant consonant sounds; in CVC words the first and last letters)

- Some CVC words and key sight words spelled correctly (use of medial vowel in CVC words)

- Simple regular words and key sight words usually spelled correctly

Left-handed children

Approximately 12% of the population are left-handed, so there's a good chance of having a few left-handers in every class of 30 children. Boys are more likely to be left-handed than girls. If a child is left-handed, any attempt to force him or her to use the right hand could cause long-term psychological damage. However, many children take quite a while working out which is their preferred hand, and some are genuinely ambidextrous. If a child seems happy to work with either hand, try gently to guide them towards the right – it's definitely easier to be right-handed in a right-handed world.

To avoid problems later, try to make special provision for left-handers in the early stages:

* Watch children carefully to gauge any genuine left-handers.

* Provide left-handed scissors so that they aren't handicapped when learning to cut out.

* When teaching handwriting movements and letter formation (see pages 82-84), don't ask them to join in with the right-handers' lessons, but provide a special lesson of their own, modelling the movement with the left hand– if there's a left-handed adult to model for them, that's ideal, but otherwise someone will have to train themselves to teach the movements left-handed.

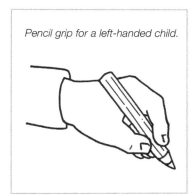

Pencil grip for a left-handed child.

* When teaching pencil grip and handwriting, again model everything for them using the left-hand.

* Provide opportunities for left-handers to talk about any difficulties.

* Some left-handers kneel up to write, because it helps them see what they're doing. An alternative is to provide a slanted 'writing block' which raises the paper above their hand.

* Ensure left-handers are seated so there is space on their left-hand side – otherwise they tend to collide with right-handers coming from the opposite direction!

* Equipment including pencil grips, writing blocks, a video demonstrating practice, and advice on the teaching of handwriting are available from Anything Lefthanded (see Resources list on page 136).

Foundations of Literacy © Sue Palmer, Featherstone Education

Audit sheet for practitioners working with three- to four-year-olds

Listening

daily activities to improve discrimination ☐

daily activities to develop social listening skills ☐

daily activities to increase attention span
(overlap with music and storytime) ☐

daily activities to develop auditory memory
(overlap with music and storytime) ☐

Talk

daily spoken language activities, including
repeating and innovating on sentences ☐

daily targeting of selected vocabulary
(changed weekly) ☐

targeting of PREPARE expressive language
in teacher- and child-initiated activities ☐

daily conversations compensating for
language delay ☐

daily talk during child-initiated activities ☐

Music

daily opportunities to keep a steady beat ☐

daily opportunities to sing (and learn) songs,
action songs and rhymes ☐

frequent opportunities to move rhythmically
(for example marching, dancing) ☐

Storytime

'five a day' reading of storybooks ☐

frequent storytelling sessions ☐

regular opportunities for children to
make up stories ☐

Print

occasional environmental print walks ☐

environmental print displayed (and
discussed) in classroom ☐

appropriate environmental print in
role-play areas ☐

frequent singing of alphabet song,
linked to chart ☐

regular activities with letters
(including writing name) ☐

occasional demonstration of different types
of reading ☐

Phonics

daily rhyme, rhythm and song (link to music) ☐

daily rhyming activities ☐

Writing

daily activities available to develop gross,
medium and fine motor skills ☐

large-scale handwriting movement activities
(link to music, drama, art) ☐

attention to pencil grip when children
use pencils ☐

occasional relevant shared writing ☐

Foundations of Literacy © Sue Palmer, Featherstone Education

Audit sheet for practitioners working with four- to five-year-olds

Listening

daily activities to improve discrimination ☐

daily activities to develop social listening skills ☐

daily activities to increase attention span
(overlap with music, storytime, phonics) ☐

daily activities to develop auditory memory
(overlap with music, storytime, phonics) ☐

weekly learning of a simple rhyme ☐

Talk

daily spoken language activities, including
repeating and innovating on sentences ☐

daily targeting of selected vocabulary
(changed weekly) ☐

daily targeting of PREPARE expressive
language ☐

daily activities to compensate for language
delay ☐

daily talk during child-initiated activities ☐

Music

regular opportunities to develop steady
beat and rhythm ☐

daily opportunities to sing (and learn) songs,
action songs and rhymes ☐

frequent opportunities to move rhythmically
(for example marching, dancing) ☐

Storytime

'five a day' reading of storybooks ☐

frequent storytelling sessions ☐

frequent opportunities for children to join in
with/recite familiar stories ☐

regular opportunities for children to
make up stories ☐

Print

frequent attention to environmental print ☐

environmental print in all role-play areas ☐

gradual linking of alphabet knowledge to
phonics ☐

demonstration of different types of reading ☐

Phonics

daily rhyme, rhythm and song
(link to music) ☐

daily oral activities to learn phonemes
and use them to segment and blend ☐

later, daily phonic activities, using magnetic
letters, etc. ☐

later, integration of phonic knowledge into
shared writing ☐

Writing

frequent large-scale practice of
letter formation ☐

later, linking letter-formation to phonics ☐

constant attention to pencil grip and
handedness ☐

daily shared writing ☐

Audit sheet for practitioners working with five- to six-year-olds

Listening

daily activities to develop attention span, auditory memory (overlap with music, storytime, phonics) ☐

weekly learning of a simple rhyme ☐

Talk

daily spoken language activities, inc repeating and innovating on sentences (circle time, storytime) daily targeting of selected vocabulary ☐

daily targeting of PREPARE expressive language ☐

daily activities to compensate for language delay ☐

Music

daily opportunities to sing (and learn) songs, action songs and rhymes ☐

frequent opportunities to move rhythmically (for example marching, dancing) ☐

Storytime

'five a day' reading of storybooks ☐

frequent storytelling sessions, with emphasis on children's retelling of stories ☐

regular opportunities for children to make up stories orally ☐

Print

frequent attention to environmental print ☐

environmental print in all role-play areas ☐

gradual linking of alphabet knowledge to phonics ☐

demonstration of different types of reading ☐

later (when phonics well established) sight word activities ☐

Phonics

daily rhyme, rhythm and song (link to music) ☐

daily phonic activities, using magnetic letters, etc. and linking to letter-formation ☐

occasional reading, when children are ready, of phonically-regular material ☐

integration of phonic knowledge into shared writing ☐

Writing

frequent practice of letter formation ☐

attention to pencil grip and handedness ☐

daily shared writing ☐

Foundations of Literacy © Sue Palmer, Featherstone Education

Phonics

As we hope is clear from *Tuning into Sound* and *Switching on the Searchlights*, we are thoroughly in favour of the teaching of phonics 'first and fast', as long as the teaching is also fun and developmentally appropriate. The developmental stages listed on page 78 were described to us by Professor Margaret Snowling, the UK's foremost expert on dyslexia, and do not vary over time. Children with no awareness of rhyme and alliteration are unlikely to benefit from systematic structured phonics teaching.

In the Appendix to the *Rose Report* (2006), there is a very helpful diagram by Dr Morag Stuart, showing the interrelationship between rapid 'word recognition' (by which she means the ability to rapidly synthesize an unfamiliar word from its phonetic elements: /b/ /a/ /sh/ → 'bash') and language comprehension (implicit in the level of children's command of spoken language). If children have good phonics skills and good spoken language they will, almost inevitably, be good readers.

However, those children with good command of spoken language but poor phonics skills will probably fall into the trap of guessing unknown words. This is not a great handicap in the early stages of reading, as a bright child can usually make pretty effective guesses, but as time goes on and the level of vocabulary becomes more difficult, guessing doesn't work. Unfortunately, the child who has learned to guess usually finds it very difficult to slow down his or her brain sufficiently to acquire the skills of decoding.

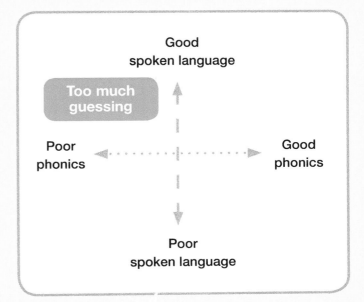

Foundations of Literacy © Sue Palmer, Featherstone Education

Children whose ability to blend and segment words is impaired for physiological reasons find it difficult to learn phonics, and – if their spoken language is good – often become inveterate guessers. When their reading doesn't progress beyond a very basic they're usually described as dyslexic. But, if phonics is not taught first and fast, children with no physiological difficulties may also learn to guess, and may be unwilling to slow down their brains at a later date to learn to decode – we could call this 'acquired dyslexia'. It is likely that, in the recent past, when phonics was taught sketchily or inappropriately (or not taught at all), many children – especially boys – suffered from acquired dyslexia. It's therefore essential that, to avoid the artificial creation of reading problems, we ensure that children are taught phonics, and taught it well, before being expected to read complex texts and write at any length.

On the other hand, if a child has poor spoken language but good phonic knowledge, he or she will be able to decode but without comprehension. As it's impossible truly to 'read' a text without understanding its meaning, this child will struggle in literacy lessons and will usually lose interest in the activity. This used to happen regularly in the 1960s and 1970s when phonics was taught thoroughly, and the children concerned were said to be 'barking at print'.

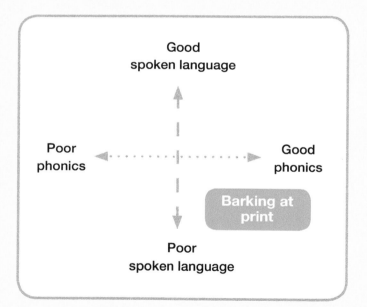

Indeed, it was because so many children from language-poor homes were found to be 'barking at print' that confidence in phonics as a teaching method waned, and it was thrown out of favour in the1970s and 1980s. Unless we concentrate on the development of speaking and listening skills as well as phonics, such children are always likely to struggle with reading.

In Scotland, where several local authorities have been teaching systematic synthetic phonics for years, many 11-year-olds from disadvantaged homes do not progress beyond a nine-year-old reading level, even on a phonic test – i.e. they are not independent readers. (Interestingly, children who started school early and were thus subjected to phonics teaching from the age of four often do not even attain nine-year-old levels of competence by their eleventh year – as one headteacher put it 'they seem to be inevitably among the failures'.)

The most comprehensive failures, of course, are the children who have neither well-developed spoken language nor phonic skill. They need early identification and special needs input.

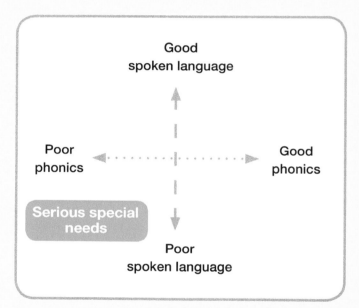

Given that practitioners are aware of the complex relationship between phonics and proficiency in spoken language (and the overarching importance of developing language competence as a whole), we believe the points listed below are essential if children are to become proficient in literacy skills.

One very important point is that you can teach phonics for reading without expecting children to write the letters. This releases them from the extra physical and cognitive load of wielding a pencil, and gives time to develop pencil control before revising phonic knowledge through the kinaesthetic channel at a later date.

Preparing for phonics

Children must be able to discriminate the phonemes of English in order to read.

Babies are born with the potential to speak any language, but during the first year or so their ears tune into the sounds of their mother tongue, and they become less able to discriminate other sounds. (That's why it's so difficult for Chinese people to pronounce the 'r' sound, which we take for granted – their brains have screened it out of their phonological range.)

So before children start learning to read, they need lots of exposure to spoken language, to ensure they can discriminate all the sounds – and, in terms of phonics, the first couple of years are very important. Three steps you can take to help this along are:

- Make sure parents know the huge importance of talking to their babies. There are downloadable parents' advice sheets at **www.wordsforlife.org.uk/** an excellent website run by the National Literacy Trust.

- Encourage parents to sing the old nursery rhymes, which emphasize specific sounds (**J**ack and **J**ill, **R**ing a **R**ing a **R**oses). The reason they've come down through the centuries is that they work.

- If you're in contact with local Sure Start units and day nurseries make sure they know the huge importance of talking, singing and rhyming with small children.

Phonics for reading

Reading an alphabetic language like English involves two key phonic skills:

- knowing that letters (and groups of letters, such as *ch* and *igh*) represent phonemes

- segmenting words into phonemes (/k/ /a/ /t/) and blending them back into words (cat)

There's growing evidence that the best approach is to teach phonics *before* starting children on formal reading instruction. But that doesn't mean starting phonics earlier – it means putting off formal reading till later. There are many other important elements in an early years curriculum – including the other six strands of *Foundations of Literacy* – so please don't start phonics teaching until you know children are ready to benefit from it. The key messages in our *Tuning into sound* chapter are:

- Ensure plenty of preliminary phonological and phonemic awareness activities (see pages 75-76) – these should also continue alongside phonics teaching.

- A 'phonics first, fast and fun' approach, using games and concrete materials, will then develop key phonic skills (but remember to keep it within the context of good early years practice).

- If something stops being fun, stop doing it! Find another way.

- Don't confuse children by simultaneously teaching phonically-irregular sight words.

- Read to children (you can't do enough of this) but save shared and guided reading and reading schemes until you've established the key phonic skills.

- Teach phonics in short sharp bursts (no more than a total of 20 minutes in a single day) which are fun, fast, multisensory and cumulative.

- Use an established scheme or put your own system together but be sure to cover the phonemes systematically, with plenty of repetition.

- Do use your professional judgement about what is appropriate for particular children – if a child is not developmentally ready to learn from an activity, it will do more harm than good.

Time spent laying the phonic foundations for reading pays off. Good phonic skills make reading 'easy', so children are more likely to succeed and make rapid progress. Explain this to parents if they start hankering for 'reading books' – *Flying Start with Literacy* by Ros Bayley and Lynn Broadbent should be helpful here. We think Year 1 is quite early enough to start shared, guided and independent reading.

Phonics for writing

Children need to encode words when they write. As English spelling is so complex, phonics for writing takes a long time to teach.

Writing involves a much wider range of skills, concepts and cognition than reading (including hand-eye coordination and fine motor control, which are very demanding for young children, especially boys). Pre-writing skills can be developed alongside 'phonics for reading':

- When you teach letter-sound correspondences, and show how to segment and blend words, children don't need to write the letters. They can demonstrate their increasing competence in encoding by using concrete materials, such as letter cards, magnetic letters or phonix cubes. Alongside these activities, you can prepare them for handwriting with something like WriteDance (Sage Publishing).

- As children's phonic knowledge develops, demonstrate how phonics helps you encode words during shared writing. Their developing grasp of phonics will probably show through in emergent writing during role-play, in the writing corner, etc. (See Appendix 5.) Give praise and appropriate support when this happens.

- When you're confident that children are ready for handwriting, use writing practice as an opportunity to revise phonic knowledge already acquired through oral lessons and the use of concrete materials.

Phonic problems

Children who have problems with phonics can often be helped through early identification and phonological training.

Research suggests most reading difficulties are caused by faulty phonological processing, due to neurological problems (often genetic) or inadequate language exposure in very early childhood. The Learning to listen and Music, movement and memory strands of *Foundations of Literacy* are therefore very important for phonics.

Schools need to spot problems and provide appropriate help before children fail at reading and fall behind. This is another good reason for putting off formal reading instruction until children are in Year 1. Ways of putting this research into practice are in their infancy, but key points seem to be:

- When you start phonics in Reception, watch for children who don't catch on as fast as the rest of the class, especially in 'segmenting and blending'.

- These children need screening for specific phonological problems. They are likely to benefit from intensive, individual help:

  - to identify the phonemes they cannot discriminate

  - to train them to hear these sounds and link them to letters.

Practice Guidance for the Early Years Foundation Stage and *Foundations of Literacy*

In this section we have cross-referenced the seven strands of *Foundations of Literacy* to:

- the developmental descriptors for three to five year-olds in 'A Unique Child' (as given in Development Matters in the EYFS, produced by Early Education) which are **non-statutory**

- the early learning goals for five-year-olds in the revised EYFS, which is a statutory document.

■	Learning to listen
■	Time to talk
■	Music, movement and memory
■	Storytime
■	Learning about print
■	Tuning into sound
■	Moving into writing

Prime areas of learning and development:

- Personal, social and emotional development
- Communication and language
- Physical development

Specific areas of learning and development:

- Literacy
- Mathematics
- Understanding the world
- Expressive arts and design

Personal, social and emotional development

Making relationships

30–50 months

- can play in a group extending and elaborating play ideas .... ■ ■
- initiate play, offering cues to peers to join them .... ■ ■
- keeps play going by responding to what others are saying or doing .... ■ ■
- demonstrates friendly behaviour, initiating conversations and forming good relationships with peers and familiar adults .... ■ ■

40–60+ months

- initiates conversations, attends to and takes account of what others say .... ■ ■
- explains own knowledge and understanding, and asks appropriate questions of others .... ■ ■
- takes steps to resolve conflict with other children .... ■ ■

ELG

- Children play cooperatively, taking turns with others .... ■ ■
- They take account of one another's ideas about how to organize their activity. .... ■ ■
- They show sensitivity to others' needs and feelings, and form positive relationships with adults and other children. .... ■ ■

Personal, social and emotional development contd.

Self-confidence and self-awareness

30–50 months

- can select and use activities and resources with help .... ▪ ▪
- welcomes and values praise for what they have done .... ▪ ▪
- enjoys responsibility of carrying out small tasks .... ▪ ▪
- is more outgoing towards unfamiliar people and more confident in new social situations .... ▪ ▪
- confident to talk to other children when playing, and will communicate freely
  about own home and community .... ▪ ▪
- shows confidence in asking adults for help .... ▪ ▪

40–60+ months

- confident to speak to others about own needs, wants, interests and opinions .... ▪ ▪
- can describe self in positive terms and talk about abilities .... ▪ ▪

ELG

- Children are confident to try new activities, and say why they like some activities
  more than others .... ▪ ▪
- They are confident to speak in a familiar group, will talk about their ideas, and will
  choose the resources they need for their chosen activities .... ▪ ▪
- They say when they do or don't need help .... ▪ ▪

Foundations of Literacy © Sue Palmer, Featherstone Education

Personal, social and emotional development contd.

Managing feelings and behaviour

30–50 months

- Aware of own feelings, and knows that some actions and words can hurt others' feelings .... ■ ■

- Begins to accept the needs of others and can take turns and share resources,
  sometimes with support from others .... ■ ■

- Can usually tolerate delay when needs are not immediately met, and understand
  wishes may not always be met .... ■ ■

- Can usually adapt behaviour to different events, social situations and changes in routines. .... ■ ■

40-60+ months

- understands that own actions affect other people .... ■ ■

- aware of the boundaries set, and of behavioural expectations in the setting ....

- beginning to be able to negotiate and solve problems without aggression .... ■ ■

ELG

- Children talk about how they and others show feelings, talk about their own and others' behaviour,
  and its consequences, and know that some behaviour is unacceptable .... ■ ■

- They work as part of a group or class, and understand and follow rules .... ■ ■

- They adjust their behaviour to different situations, and take changes of routine in their stride .... ■ ■

Foundations of Literacy © Sue Palmer, Featherstone Education

Communication and language

Listening and attention

30–50 months

- listens to others one-to-one or in small groups, when conversation interests them .... ▪
- listens to stories with increasing attention and recall .... ▪
- joins in with repeated refrains and anticipates key events and phrases in rhymes and stories... ▪ ▪ ▫ ▪
- focusing attention – still listen or do, but can shift own attention... ▪
- is able to follow directions (if not intently focused on own choice of activity) .... ▪ ▫

40–60+ months

- maintains attention, concentrates and sits quietly during appropriate activity.............................. ▪
- two-channelled attention – can listen and do for short span.. ▪

ELG

- Children listen attentively in a range of situations... ▪
- They listen to stories, accurately anticipating key events and respond to what they hear with relevant comments, questions or actions .... ▪ ▪ ▫ ▪
- They give their attention to what others say, and respond appropriately, while engaged in another activity .... ▪ ▪

Understanding

30–50 months

- understands use of objects... ▪
- shows understanding of prepositions, such as 'under', 'on top', 'behind', by carrying out an action or selecting correct picture .... ▪ ▪
- responds to simple instructions... ▪ ▪
- beginning to understand 'why' and 'how' questions .... ▪ ▪

40–60+ months

- responds to instructions involving a two-part sequence .... ▪ ▪
- understands humour, e.g. nonsense rhymes and jokes .... ▪ ▫ ▫ ▪
- able to follow a story without pictures or props.. ▪ ▪
- listens and responds to ideas expressed by others in conversation or discussion....................... ▪ ▪

ELG

- Children follow instructions involving several ideas or actions.. ▪
- They answer 'how' and 'why' questions about their experiences and in response to stories or events... ▪ ▪ ▫

Communication and language contd.

Speaking

30–50 months

- beginning to use more complex sentences to link thoughts, e.g. using 'and', 'because' ....
- can retell a simple past event in correct order ....
- uses talk to connect ideas, explain what is happening and anticipate what might happen next, recall and relive past experiences ....
- questions why things happen and gives explanations – asks, e.g. 'who', 'what', 'when', 'how' ....
- uses a range of tenses (verb forms), e.g. play, playing, will play, played ....
- uses intonation, rhythm and phrasing to make meaning clear to others ....
- uses vocabulary focused on objects and people that are of particular importance to them ....
- builds up vocabulary that reflects the breadth of their experiences ....
- uses talk in pretending that objects stand for something else in play, e.g. 'This box is my castle' ....

40–60+ months

- extends vocabulary, especially by grouping and naming, exploring the meaning and sounds of new words ....
- uses language to imagine and recreate roles and experiences in play situations ....
- links statements and sticks to a main theme or intention ....
- uses talk to organize, sequence and clarify thinking, ideas, feelings and events...
- introduces a storyline or narrative into their play ....

ELG

- Children express themselves effectively, showing awareness of listeners' needs ....
- They use past, present and future forms accurately when talking about events that have happened or are to happen in the future...
- They develop their own narratives and explanations by connecting ideas or events...................................

Moving and handling

30–50 months

- moves freely and with pleasure and confidence in a range of ways, such as slithering, shuffling, rolling, crawling, walking, running, jumping, skipping, sliding and hopping ....
- mounts stairs, steps or climbing equipment using alternate feet ....
- walks downstairs, two feet to each step while carrying a small object ....
- runs skilfully and negotiates space successfully, adjusting speed or direction to avoid obstacles ....
- can stand momentarily on one foot when shown ....
- can catch a large ball ....
- draws lines and circles using gross motor movements ....
- uses one-handed tools and equipment, e.g. makes snips in paper with child scissors ....
- holds pencil between thumb and two fingers, no longer using whole-hand grasp ....
- holds pencil near point near point between first two fingers and thumb, and uses it with good control ....
- can copy some letters, e.g. letters from their name ....

40–60+ months

- experiments with different ways of moving ....
- jumps off an object and lands appropriately ....
- negotiates space successfully when playing racing and chasing games with other children, adjusting speed or changing direction to avoid obstacles ....
- travels with confidence and skill around, under, over and through balancing and climbing equipment ....
- shows increasing control over an object in pushing, patting, throwing, catching or kicking it ....
- uses simple tools to effect changes to materials ....
- handles tools, objects, construction and malleable materials safely and with increasing control ....
- shows a preference for a dominant hand ....
- begins to use anti-clockwise movement and retrace vertical lines ....
- begins to form recognizable letters ....
- uses a pencil and holds it effectively to form recognizable letters, most of which are correctly formed ....

ELG

- Children show good control and coordination in large and small movements ....
- They move confidently in a range of ways, safely negotiating space ....
- They handle equipment and tools effectively, including pencils for writing ....

Physical development contd.

Health and self-care

30–50 months

- can tell adults when hungry or tired or when they want to rest or play .... ■
- can observe the effects of activity on their bodies ....
- understands that equipment and tools have to be used safely...
- gains more bowel and bladder control and can attend to toileting needs most of the time themselves ....
- can usually manage washing and drying hands ....
- dresses with help ....

40–60+ months

- eats a healthy range of foodstuffs and understands need for variety in food ....
- usually dry and clean during the day ....
- shows some understanding that good practices with regard to exercise, eating, sleeping and hygiene can contribute to good health..
- shows understanding of the need for safety when tackling new challenges and considers and manages some risks..
- shows understanding of how to transport and store equipment safely................................
- practises some appropriate safety measures without direct supervision.............................

ELG

- Children know the importance for good health of physical exercise and a healthy diet, and talk about ways to keep healthy and safe. .... ■
- They manage their own basic hygiene and personal needs successfully, including dressing and going to the toilet independently..

Specific areas: Literacy

Reading

30–50 months

- enjoys rhyming and rhythmic activities ....
- shows awareness of rhyme and alliteration ....
- recognizes rhythm in spoken words ....
- listens to and joins in with stories and poems, one-to-one and also in small groups ....
- joins in with repeated refrains and anticipates key events and phrases in rhymes and stories..
- beginning to be aware of the way stories are structured...
- suggests how the story might end...
- listens to stories with increasing attention and recall ....
- describes main story settings, events and principle characters......................................
- shows interest in illustrations and print in books and print in the environment................
- recognizes familiar words and signs, such as own name and advertising logos ....
- looks at books independently ....
- handles books carefully ....
- knows information can be relayed in the form of print..
- holds books the correct way up and turns pages ....
- knows that print carries meaning and, in English, is read from left to right and top to bottom ....

40–60+ months

- continues a rhyming string...
- hears and says the initial sound in words ....
- can segment the sounds in simple words and blend them together and knows which letters represent some of them...
- links sounds to letters, naming and sounding the letters of the alphabet ....
- begins to read words and simple sentences ....
- uses vocabulary and forms of speech that are increasingly influenced by their experiences of books..
- enjoys an increasing range of books ....
- knows that information can be retrieved from books and computers ....

ELG

- Children read and understand simple sentences...
- They use phonic knowledge to decode regular words and read them aloud accurately ....
- They also read some common irregular words...
- They demonstrate understanding when talking with others about what they have read ....

Literacy contd.

Literacy

Writing

30–50 months

- sometimes gives meaning to marks as they draw and paint .... ▨ ▩
- ascribes meanings to marks that they see in different places. .... ▨ ▩

40–60+ months

- gives meaning to marks they make as they draw, write and paint .... ▨ ▩ ▩
- begins to break the flow of speech into words .... ▩
- continues a rhyming string .... ▩ ▩ ▢
- hears and says the initial sound in words .... ▩ ▩
- can segment the sounds in simple words and blend them together .... ▨ ▢ ▩
- links sounds to letters, naming and sounding the letters of the alphabet .... ▨ ▢ ▩ ▩ ▩
- uses some clearly identifiable letters to communicate meaning, representing some sounds correctly and in sequence .... ▨ ▩ ▩
- writes own name and other things such as labels, captions .... ▨ ▩ ▩
- attempts to write short sentences in meaningful contexts .... ▨ ▩ ▩

ELG

- Children use their phonic knowledge to write words in ways which match their spoken sounds .... ▨ ▩ ▩
- They also write some irregular common words .... ▨ ▩
- They write simple sentences which can be read by themselves and others .... ▨ ▩ ▩
- Some words are spelled correctly and others are phonetically plausible ....

Foundations of Literacy © Sue Palmer, Featherstone Education

Appendices 127

Mathematics

Numbers

30–50 months

- uses some number names and number language spontaneously .... ■
- uses some number names accurately in play .... ■
- recites numbers in order to ten .... ■
- knows that numbers identify how many objects are in a set .... ■
- beginning to represent numbers using fingers, marks on paper or pictures .... ■
- sometimes matches numeral and quantity correctly ....
- shows curiosity about numbers by offering comments or asking questions .... ■
- compares two groups of objects, saying when they have the same number .... ■
- shows an interest in number problems ....
- separates a group of three or four objects in different ways, beginning to recognize that the total is still the same ....
- shows an interest in numerals in the environment .... ■
- shows an interest in representing numbers .... ■
- realizes not only objects, but anything, can be counted, including steps, claps, or jumps ....

40–60+ months

- recognizes some numerals of personal significance .... ■
- recognizes numerals 1 to 5 .... ■
- counts up to three or four objects by saying one number name for each item .... ■
- counts actions or objects which cannot be moved .... ■
- counts objects to ten, and beginning to count beyond ten .... ■
- counts out up to six objects from a larger group .... ■
- selects the correct numeral to represent one to five, then one to ten objects ....
- counts an irregular arrangement of up to ten objects .... ■
- estimates how many objects they can see and checks by counting them .... ■
- uses the language of 'more' and 'fewer' to compare two sets of objects .... ■
- finds the total number of items in two groups by counting all of them .... ■
- says the number that is one more than a given number .... ■
- finds one more or one less from a group of up to five objects, then ten objects .... ■
- in practical activities and discussion, begins to use the vocabulary involved in adding and subtracting .... ■
- records, using marks that they can interpret and explain .... ■ ■
- begins to identify own mathematical problems based on own interests and fascinations .... ■

ELG

- Children count reliably with numbers from one to 20, place them in order and say which number is one more or one less than a given number .... ■ ■
- Using quantities and objects, they add and subtract two single-digit numbers and count on or back to find the answer .... ■ ■
- They solve problems, including doubling, halving and sharing .... ■ ■

Foundations of Literacy © Sue Palmer, Featherstone Education

Mathematics contd.

Shape, space and measure

30–50 months

- shows an interest in shape and space by playing with shapes or making arrangements with objects ....
- shows awareness of similarities of shapes in the environment ....
- uses positional language...
- shows interest in shape by sustained construction activity or by talking about shapes or arrangements ....
- shows interest in shapes in the environment ....
- uses shapes appropriately for tasks ....
- beginning to talk about the shapes of everyday objects, e.g. round, tall ....

40–60+ months

- beginning to use mathematical names for 'solid' 3D shapes and 'flat' 2D shapes, and mathematical terms to describe shapes...
- selects a particular named shape ....
- can describe their relative position, such as behind or next to ....
- orders two or three items by length or height...
- orders two items by weight or capacity ....
- uses familiar objects and common shapes to create and recreate patterns and build models ....
- uses everyday language related to time ....
- beginning to use everyday language related to money ....
- orders and sequences familiar events ....
- measures short periods of time in simple ways...

ELG

- Children use everyday language to talk about size, weight, capacity, position, distance, time and money to compare quantities and objects and to solve problems.....................................
- They recognize, create and describe patterns..
- They explore characteristics of everyday objects and shapes and use mathematical language to describe them ....

Understanding the world

People and communities

30–50 months

- shows interest in the lives of people who are familiar to them .... ■

- remembers and talks about significant events in their own experience .... ■

- recognizes and describes special times or events for family or friends .... ■

- shows interest in different occupations and ways of life .... ■

- knows some of the things that make them unique, and can talk about some of the similarities and differences in relation to friends or family .... ■

40–60+ months

- enjoys joining in with family customs and routines..

ELG

- Children talk about past and present events in their own lives and in the lives of family members.. ■ ■

- They know that other children don't always enjoy the same things, and are sensitive to this .... ■ ■

- They know about similarities and differences between themselves and others, and among families, communities and traditions .... ■ ■

Foundations of Literacy © Sue Palmer, Featherstone Education

Understanding the world contd.

The world

30–50 months

- comments and asks questions about aspects of their familiar world, such as the place where they live or the natural world .... ▪
- can talk about some of the things they have observed, such as plants, animals, natural and found objects .... ▪
- talks about why things happen and how things work.. ▪
- developing an understanding of growth, decay and changes over time.............................. ▪
- shows care and concern for living things and the environment .... ▪

40–60+ months

- looks closely at similarities, differences, patterns and change...................................... ▪

ELG

- Children know about similarities and differences in relation to places, objects, materials and living things.. ▪
- They talk about the features of their own immediate environment and how environments might vary from one another .... ▪
- They make observations of animals and plants and explain why some things occur, and talk about changes.. ▪

Technology

30–50 months

- knows how to operate simple equipment, e.g. turns on CD player and uses remote control... ▪
- shows an interest in technological toys with knobs or pulleys, or real objects such as cameras or mobile phones .... ▪
- shows skill in making toys work by pressing parts or lifting flaps to achieve effects such as sound, movements or new images.. ▪
- knows that information can be retrieved from computers .... ▪

40–60+ months

- completes a simple program on a computer .... ▪
- uses ICT hardware to interact with age-appropriate computer software ....

ELG

- Children recognize that a range of technology is used in places such as homes .... and schools...
- They select and use technology for particular purposes ....

Expressive arts and design

Exploring and using media and materials

30–50 months

- enjoys joining in with dancing and ring games .... ☐
- sings a few familiar songs .... ☐
- beginning to move rhythmically .... ☐
- imitates movement in response to music .... ☐
- taps out simple repeated rhymes .... ☐
- explores and learns how sounds can be changed .... ☐
- explores colour and how colours can be changed .... ☐
- understands that they can use lines to enclose a space, and then begin to use these shapes to represent objects .... ☐
- begins to be interested in and describe the texture of things .... ☐
- uses various construction materials .... ☐
- beginning to construct, stacking blocks vertically and horizontally, making enclosures and creating spaces .... ☐
- joins construction pieces together to build and balance .... ☐
- realises tools can be used for a purpose .... ☐

40–60+ months

- begins to build a repertoire of songs and dances .... ☐
- explores the different sounds of instruments .... ☐
- explores what happens when they mix colours .... ☐
- experiments to create different textures .... ☐
- understands that different media can be combined to create new effects .... ☐
- manipulates materials to achieve a planned effect .... ☐
- constructs with a purpose in mind, using a variety of resources .... ☐
- uses simple tools and techniques competently and appropriately .... ☐
- selects appropriate resources and adapts when necessary .... ☐
- selects tools and techniques needed to shape, assemble and join materials they are using .... ☐

ELG

- Children sing songs, make music and dance, and experiment with ways of changing them .... ☐
- They safely use and explore a variety of materials, tools and techniques, experimenting with colour, design, texture, form and function .... ☐

Expressive arts and design contd.

Being imaginative

30–50 months

- developing preferences for forms of expression...
- uses movement to express feelings..
- creates movement in response to music ....
- sings to self and makes up simple songs ....
- makes up rhythms..
- notices what adults do, imitating what is observed and then doing it spontaneously when the adult is not there..
- engages in imaginative role-play based on own first-hand experiences............................
- builds stories around toys, e.g. farm animals needing rescue from an armchair 'cliff'.....
- uses available resources to create props to support role-play..
- captures experiences and responses with a range of media, such as music, dance and paint and other materials or words ....

40–60+ months

- creates simple representations of events, people and objects..
- initiates new combinations of movement and gesture in order to express and respond to feelings, ideas and experiences..
- chooses particular colours to use for a purpose ....
- introduces a storyline or narrative into their play ....
- plays alongside other children who are engaged in the same theme................................
- plays cooperatively as part of a group to develop and act out a narrative.......................

ELG

- Children use what they have learned about media and materials in original ways, thinking about uses and purposes..
- They represent their own ideas, thoughts and feelings through design and technology, art, music, dance, role-play and stories..

Further reading

Babytalk Sally Ward (New Century)

Basic Timing and Child Development Kristyn Kuhlmen and Lawrence J Schweinhart (High/Scope Educational Research Foundation Ypsilanti, Michigan, 2000)

Child-Initiated Learning: Hundreds of ideas for independent learning in the early years Ros Bayley and Sally Featherstone (Featherstone, Bloomsbury Publishing, 2013)

Communicative Musicality: exploring the basis of human companionship, Stephen Malloch and Colwyn Trevarthen (Oxford University Press,2010)

Development Matters in the Early Years Foundation Stage (Early Education, 2012)

Exploring Writing and Play in the Early Years, Nigel Hall and Anne Robinson (David Fulton, 2003)

Hopping Home Backwards – Body Intelligence and Movement Play Penny Greenland (Jabadao, 2000)

Getting ready for phonics Ros Bayley, Helen Bilton, Lynn Broadbent, Marion Dowling, Margaret Edgington, Janet Evans, Jennie Lindon, Judith Harries and Linda Pound (Featherstone, Bloomsbury Publishing, 2013)

Letters and Sounds (DfES, 2007)

Not Just Talking: Identifying Non-verbal Communication Difficulties - A Life Changing Approach Sioban Boyce (Speechmark, 2012)

Statutory Framework for the Early Years Foundation Stage (Department for Education, 2012)

Supporting Musical Development in the Early Years, Linda Pound and Chris Harrison (Open University Press, 2002)

The Scientist in the Crib: what early learning tells us about the mind Alison Gopnik, Andrew N Meltzoff, Patricia K Kuhl (Harper Collins 2011)

The Cradle of Thought: exploring the origins of thinking Peter Hobson (Pan 2007)

The Boy Who Would Be A Helicopter and other books, Vivian Gussin Paley (Harvard University Press, 1991)

The Education of Six-Year-Olds in England, Denmark and Finland, (HMI, 2003)

Toxic Childhood: How The Modern World Is Damaging Our Children And What We Can Do About It Sue Palmer (Orion, 2007)

21st Century Boys How Modern Life Can Drive Them off the Rails and How to Get Them Back on Track Sue Palmer (Orion, 2010)

21st Century Girls: how female minds develop, how to raise bright balanced girls, and why the world needs them more than ever Sue Palmer (Orion, 2013)

Too Much Too Soon: the erosion of early childhood edited by Richard House (Hawthorn Press, 2011)

Too Much Too Soon video of European Early Years Practice, Clare and David Mills, available on YouTube

Unhurried Pathways – a new framework for early childhood practice Early Childhood Action, 2012 (www.earlychildhoodaction.com)

Flying Start With Literacy: activities for parents and children Ros Bayley and Lynn Broadbent (Network Continuum)

Foundations of Literacy © Sue Palmer, Featherstone Education

Recommended resources

Learning to listen

Helping Young Children To Listen and Helping Young Children to Concentrate Ros Bayley and Lynn Broadbent (Lawrence Educational Publications: www.lawrenceeducational.co.uk)

The Little Book of Listening Clare Beswick (Featherstone Education: 01858 881212)

You Can Teach Your Class to Listen: Ages 4–7 Sue Palmer (Scholastic 2007)

Language through Listening Becky Shanks and Visual Cue Cards – 12 page pack (Black Sheep Publishing: 01535 631 356)

Picture Communication System (PCS) pictures and symbols (www.pecs.com)

There are many games on the market (using ready-made taped sounds) such as: *Picture Sound Lotto* for age 4-8 (LDA: 0845 120 4776), *Soundtracks* for age 3-6 (from Living and Learning/Galt available in toy shops and from online suppliers)

For parents: *Talk to your Baby* (National Literacy Trust: www.literacytrust.org.uk, www.wordsforlife.org.uk)

Time to talk

Talking Point website by ICAN, the speech and language charity www.talkingpoint.org.uk

Resources from the *Hello* campaign, run by the Communication Trust www.thecommunicationtrust.org.uk

Time to Talk Alison Schroeder (LDA www.ldalearning.com)

Helping Young Children to Speak with Confidence Ros Bayley, Lynn Broadbent and Andrina Flinders; *The Super Vaky Pack* Ros Bayley and Lynn Broadbent (Lawrence Educational Publications: www.lawrenceeducational.co.uk)

Nursery Narrative Pack and Reception Narrative Pack Becky Shanks (Black Sheep Publishing: www.blacksheeppress.co.uk)

Little Book of Prop Boxes for Role-play and other little books (Featherstone, Bloomsbury Publishing)

Feeling Spinners/Circle Time sentence starts/barrier game materials/masks & puppets/feely bag, etc. (TTS www.tts-group.co.uk)

Here we go round and other titles – Circle Time games (Positive Press: www.circle-time.co.uk)

Storyboxes and *25 Exciting Things to do with a Builder's Tray* Helen Bromley (Lawrence Educational Publications: www.lawrenceeducational.co.uk)

Spirals books and training on language development for children with language delay (Marion Nash, Jackie Lowe, et al: www.spiralstraining.co.uk)

Music, movement and memory

Helping Young Children with a steady beat Ros Bayley and Lynn Broadbent; *Ros Bayley's Wicked Action Songs*

Ros Bayley's rap books and Beat Baby materials; *Helping Young Children to Learn through Movement* Celia O'Donovan (Lawrence Educational Publications: www.lawrenceeducational.co.uk)

Carousel CDs songs for developing language skills (Linda Caroe www.carouselmusicworkshops.co.uk)

Time to Sing CD (Black Sheep Publishing: www.blacksheeppress.co.uk)

The Little Book of Music (Featherstone Education)

Sounds Like Playing Margery Ouvry (Early Education: www.earlyeducation.org.uk)

Music Express Foundation Stage (Developing Basic Music Skills); *Three Tapping Teddies*, etc (stories with music activities); *Tom Thumb's Musical Maths* and many other titles (A&C Black: www.bloomsbury.com)

Frantic Music Games for EYFS Fran Carpenter (www.franticproductions.co.uk)

Storytime!

Storylines (book) and *Angel and friends* (video) – ideas for using large puppets in storytelling activities, by Ros Bayley and Lynn Broadbent: *Almost Traditional Tales* Ros Bayley (Lawrence Educational Publications: www.lawrenceeducational.co.uk)

Speaking and Listening through Narrative Becky Shanks (Black Sheep Publishing: www.blacksheeppress.co.uk)

The Little Book of Storytelling Clare Beswick (Featherstone Education)

Storysacks materials Neil Griffiths (Storysacks Ltd: www.storysack.com)

Simply the Best: Books for 0-7 years Ann Lazim and Sue Ellis (Centre for Literacy in Primary Education www.clpe.co.uk)

Storytelling ideas from Pie Corbett for Reception and upwards: www.piecorbett.org.uk

Puppet Talk Lillian Coppock (Belair Publications)

Big book story maps, masks, storyboxes, timelines and other resources (TTS catalogue: www.tts-group.co.uk)

Learning about print

Role-play Print Packs Sue Palmer (TTS Group: www.tts-group.co.uk)

Early Vision videos for role-play, Sue Marshall (www.earlyvision.co.uk)

Writing Through Role-play Lesley Clark (Sound Learning, www.soundlearning.co.uk)

A Corner to Learn Neil Griffith (Nelson Thornes)

Tuning into sound

Helping Young Children with Phonological Awareness, Ros Bayley and Lynn Broadbent (Lawrence Educational Publications: www.lawrenceeducational.co.uk)

Bingo Lingo (songs and rhymes) Helen McGregor (A&C Black: www.bloomsbury.com)

Phonemic awareness in young children (games for developing phonemic awareness) Marilyn Jager Adams et al (Jessica Kingsley Publishers)

Rhymes (activities around well-known rhymes) Rhona Whiteford (Belair Early Years: Harper Collins Publishers)

The Kingfisher Playtime Treasury (playground rhymes and games) Pie Corbett (Kingfisher Books)

The Phonics Handbook Sue Lloyd – known as 'Jolly Phonics' (Jolly Publishing)

Sue Palmer's Synthetic Phonix cubes for blending and segmenting, Philip and Tacey, Findel Education (www.findel-education.co.uk)

Magnetic letters and other phonics resources (www.tts-group.co.uk)

Moving into writing

Write Dance in the early years (video, CD and teacher's book) – teaching handwriting through music and movement Raghild Oussoren Voors (Sage Publications: www.sagepub.com)

Penpals Foundation 1 pack – teaching book and CD (Cambridge University Press)

Let's go Zudio creative activities for dance and music, including CD (A&C Black: www.bloomsbury.com))

Reasonably priced individual whiteboards blank/widelined (www.tts-group.co.uk)

Left-handed Children video and catalogue of resources for left-handers: Anything Lefthanded www.anythinglefthanded.co.uk

JABADAO – Centre for the Study of Movement, Learning and Health: kits to support developmental movement play and other materials (www.jabadao.org)

Foundations of Literacy © Sue Palmer, Featherstone Education